Martin Dudley, Rector of St Bartho⋯⋯ ⸝⸝⸝
London since 1995, studied theolo⸝ ⸝⸝⸝g s College, London,
and voluntary sector management at the City University Cass
Business School. A Fellow of the Society of Antiquaries of London
and of the Royal Historical Society, he is also a City of London
Common Councilman, a Governor of the Museum of London, a
school governor and a charity trustee.

Virginia Rounding is a member of the PCC of St Bartholomew the
Great, where she has worked with Martin Dudley in a number of
roles over the past 12 years. In addition to the books co-authored
with Martin, she is the author of *Catherine the Great* and *Grandes
Horizontales*, and reviews regularly for a number of national
newspapers. She is currently a Royal Literary Fund Fellow at the
Courtauld Institute of Art, and Clerk to the City of London Guild
of Public Relations Practitioners.

Dudley and Rounding's *The Parish Survival Guide* was published
by SPCK in 2004, and *Serving the Parish* in 2006.

Churchwardens
A Survival Guide

Revised edition

Martin Dudley
and
Virginia Rounding

First published in Great Britain in 2003

Society for Promoting Christian Knowledge
36 Causton Street
London SW1P 4ST

Reprinted four times
Revised edition published 2009

British Library Cataloguing-in-Publication Data
A catalogue record for this book is available from the British Library

ISBN 978–0–281–06092–4

1 3 5 7 9 10 8 6 4 2

Typeset by Avocet Typeset, Chilton, Aylesbury, Bucks
Printed in Great Britain by Ashford Colour Press

Produced on paper from sustainable forests

In memoriam

David Hands QC

Contents

Acknowledgements

There are various people who have assisted us (wittingly or unwittingly) in the preparation of this book and whom we would like to thank. These include the Bishop of Oxford (when Bishop of Jarrow) for his perceptive comments on an early draft; the Parochial Church Council of St Bartholomew the Great for its contribution in addressing many of the issues discussed in our chapter 'New tasks for the twenty-first century'; Nick and Sarah Kelsey, Michael Moss, Beatrice Perch and Nicholas Riddle for the experience they have brought from their professional lives into the service of the Church; Duncan Morum and Philip Hollins, former churchwardens of St Bartholomew's, for giving proof that it is possible to survive as churchwardens and to relinquish office gracefully, and Monica Darnbrough and Ian Kelly for putting our book to the test on taking up the office of churchwarden.

Introduction

This book is intended to act as a guide both for existing church-wardens and for those considering whether to stand for election. There are approximately 26,000 churchwardens in the Church of England, and every year a proportion of these resign or retire, leaving many vacancies to be filled. Taking on the role of church-warden can be a daunting prospect, in part at least because there has been an absence of clear guidelines as to precisely what a church-warden is supposed to do. Much has been based on custom – that is, on what has been done before – and, though there are certain things a churchwarden must do (those things established by law), there are many grey areas and at times even a sense of confu-sion. Our aim in writing *Churchwardens: A Survival Guide* is to tackle the grey areas, lessen the sense of confusion and present the role of churchwarden as one that is always challenging, sometimes enjoyable, sometimes onerous, frequently rewarding – and one that may or may not be for you. If you decide – or have already decided – that it is indeed for you, then we hope that this book will assist you in undertaking the role with confidence and with an awareness of playing your part in the mission of Christ in his Church. As the author of *Hints for Churchwardens, Sidesmen and Others* wrote in 1920: 'The office of churchwarden is one of dignity and considerable antiquity. It is a position of great public utility, and, when the duties are intelligently and faithfully discharged, may be of great service in promoting the effective Church life of a parish.'

The Church of England

The Church of England may be considered in at least two ways. If it is looked at from above, it is divided into two provinces,

Canterbury and York, and into 43 dioceses, from Bath and Wells to York, which are subdivided geographically into 8,363 benefices and 13,033 parishes with 16,222 churches served by 8,724 full-time stipendiary and a very considerable number of retired, part-time and non-stipendiary clergy, readers and parish workers of many sorts. Looked at from below, the parish is the basic unit, the parishes are grouped into benefices, and the benefices into the dioceses that form the two provinces. Looked at from above, the Archbishops, the General Synod and the Church Commissioners may be the most significant, or certainly the most visible, parts of the Church. Looked at from below, the local church, parish and benefice are most visible and most important. And the most significant statistic for us is that the 13,033 parishes have more than 26,000 churchwardens! On a conservative estimate, there are three times as many churchwardens as stipendiary clergy.

Central church statistics, fascinating though they are (and available both in printed form and online), are concerned with the Church of England as a whole and tell us very little about the rich diversity of parish life. Diocesan year books often provide statistical breakdowns of electoral roll and communicant numbers, and diocesan newspapers celebrate and report many aspects of parish life. Parish websites, encouraged by the Ecclesiastical Insurance Group, provide useful, if self-selected, insights into what other parishes are trying to do. But to get a taste of the diversity of benefices and parishes, and to know something of how they see themselves, one might look at the clerical advertisements in the *Church Times*. The clergy are often asked, 'How did you come to have this job?' and the answer, very often, is, 'I saw it advertised'. In one week in October 2008 the following advertisements for clergy appeared:

1 The Parish of St Mary the Virgin, Shenfield, a suburb of Brentwood on the edge of beautiful Essex countryside, wanted a priest of breadth and maturity, at ease with the diversity of opinion within the Church today.
2 Blidworth and Rainworth, former coalfield communities in the Diocese of Southwell and Nottingham, with an electoral roll of 108, a priest colleague, readers, keen lay leaders and friendly congregations, needed a priest in charge.

3 A house-for-duty priest (without a stipend) was required for
   the four delightful small rural Norfolk villages of Smallburgh,
   Dilham, Honing and Crostwight.
4 A team rector was required for the Parish of Melton Mowbray
   in the Diocese of Leicester, with responsibility for the majestic
   parish church in the centre of the market town. This post was
   expected to attract applicants with the potential for senior
   leadership in the Church.
5 The Archdeacon of Horsham was looking for a priest for a
   benefice of two parishes, Petworth and Egdean, who would
   'walk the parish', contribute to community and ecumenical life,
   and proclaim the Gospel with both clarity and compassion.
6 Stratton, North Cerney, Baunton, and Bagendon in the Diocese
   of Gloucester, a community on the northern edge of
   Cirencester and three villages, united in a single benefice,
   needed a priest-in-charge.
7 The Team Rector of Poplar in east London was looking for a
   team vicar for St Nicholas' Church who 'despite the "ups and
   downs" will persevere and take initiative'.
8 An energetic, strategically minded priest, able to lead, enthuse
   and train others, was being sought as Deanery Missioner and
   priest-in-charge of two beautiful villages possessing medieval
   churches in Teesdale, with the added bonus that the vicarage in
   Gainford had fishing rights!
9 Stamina and vigour would be needed by the new team rector
   of the Golden Cap Team in the Sherborne Area of Salisbury
   diocese, as would a sense of humour and a deep spirituality.

This list shows something of the diversity of benefices and
parishes, ranging from the single-church suburban parish to the
twelve-parish rural benefice, and witnesses to the growing number
of team ministries as well as retirement and house-for-duty positions available to the parochial clergy. It is increasingly unlikely
that a priest will be dealing with just two churchwardens (and one
Parochial Church Council (PCC)) or that churchwardens will be
able to speak of 'our' minister, vicar or rector in an exclusive
sense. The ministry team for a parish or benefice may well include
stipendiary, non-stipendiary and retired clergy, ministers from
other denominations, readers and lay workers of many sorts, paid

and voluntary, and the churchwarden may be the man or woman on the spot carrying significant and rewarding responsibility for the local church or parish.

It may help if we understand some of the ways in which the Church of England groups parishes and benefices for administrative and pastoral purposes.

A **parish** is a geographical area, constituted for ecclesiastical purposes. An ecclesiastical parish may not be coterminous with a civil parish. A parish is normally served by a parish church. A priest can hold only one parish unless permitted to hold two or more in **plurality**.

A **benefice** means the office of **rector** or **vicar** of a parish or parishes with cure of souls (i.e. pastoral care of parishioners) but is used as a shorthand for the **area of a benefice**, meaning the parish or parishes that make up the benefice.

So, an individual parish can stand alone and be a benefice itself, or it can be united with others so that the **parishes together** form the area of the benefice. A parish has a Parochial Church Council.

An **incumbent**, known as the vicar or rector, holds the freehold of the parish or benefice (which confers certain rights on him or her) but could also be a **priest-in-charge**, who ministers under licence from the bishop.

The language becomes slightly more complicated in a **team ministry** in which one of the clergy is the **team rector** and the others are **team vicars**. Neither of these offices is normally freehold but may be described as leasehold (i.e. for a given contractual period, renewable for some further specified period). The team usually has a single PCC with the individual churches having a District Church Council (DCC).

Another type of ministry, less formal and structured than team ministry, is **group ministry**, in which a number of benefices or parishes are grouped together and may share ministries.

The benefices and parishes in a given geographical area form a **deanery**. The clergy of the deanery meet together under the chairmanship of the **rural dean** or, in cities, the **area dean**. The rural or area dean is normally appointed by the bishop after consultation with the clergy. He or she has no formal hierarchical office as such but presides over the meeting of the clergy, known as the **clergy chapter**, and chairs the **deanery synod**.

A number of deaneries make up an **archdeaconry** under an **archdeacon**, who has certain powers and responsibilities apart from those conferred or delegated by the bishop. A number of archdeaconries, usually two or three, make up a **diocese**, or, to look at it the other way, a diocese, which consists of a number of parishes, is divided into archdeaconries and deaneries. Just to add to the confusion, a diocese may have, in addition to the **diocesan bishop** (also referred to as the **Ordinary**), assistant bishops known as **suffragan bishops**. They may carry titles of parts of the diocese (such as Hertford and Bedford in the diocese of St Albans), though they do not have cathedrals in the places from which they draw their names.

Some dioceses operate a formal division of authority under the diocesan bishop known as an area system, and have **area bishops**. Oxford diocese has area bishops of Reading, Buckingham, and Dorchester, and London has area bishops of Edmonton, Stepney, Willesden and Kensington, and a suffragan bishop of Fulham.

The dioceses in the south form the **Province of Canterbury** and those in the north the **Province of York**. The two provinces make up the Church of England. The diocesan bishops together with some elected area and suffragan bishops form the **Bench of Bishops** or the **House of Bishops**.

In parallel with this is a system of government called a **synodical** system. There are three levels of synodical government: the **deanery synod**, the **diocesan synod** and the **General Synod**. The first consists of all the active clergy of the deanery and lay members elected at the annual meetings in parishes, chaired by the rural or area dean with a lay vice-chairman. The second consists of clergy and laity elected by the members of deanery synods, voting by houses (i.e. as clergy and laity separately). The General Synod consists of the House of Bishops, clergy elected by all the qualified clergy (the **House of Clergy**) and laity elected by the lay members of deanery synods (the **House of Laity**). The equivalent in the General Synod of an Act of Parliament is a **Measure** (e.g. the Churchwardens Measure 2001). A Measure, having been passed by the Synod, goes to the Ecclesiastical Committee of Parliament and through both Houses of Parliament before receiving the Royal Assent. Broadly speaking, the General Synod deals with matters of concern to the whole Church, and the diocesan synod with matters concerning the diocese (like the budget and the method of apportioning the Common Fund). The deanery deals with the implementation of decisions made higher up and passes parochial concerns upwards through the synodical system.

The cathedral church is the seat of the diocesan bishop – *cathedra* means seat or throne – and has its own structure, usually consisting of a **dean** (not to be confused with a rural dean!), canons who reside (known as **residentiary canons**), and canons who do not (known as **honorary canons** or, in some cathedrals, **prebendaries**). The bishop often honours a priest of the diocese by making him or her an honorary canon or prebendary. Each level has its own distinctive titles and, though not crucially important, it may help if we know what each means.

The Reverend is the honorific title of all the clergy

The Reverend Canon or **The Reverend Prebendary** for those
  honoured by the bishop in this way

The Reverend Canon for the residentiary canons of the
  cathedral

The Very Reverend for the cathedral's dean

The Venerable for the archdeacon

The Right Reverend for any bishop

The Most Reverend for an archbishop

The archbishops and the Bishop of London are Privy Councillors and so have the additional title **The Right Honourable,** to give **The Most Reverend and Right Honourable** for the archbishops and **The Right Reverend and Right Honourable** for the Bishop of London.

◆ 1 ◆

The office of churchwarden

Its origins and how it came about

According to the *Oxford English Dictionary* the word 'church-warden' first appeared in the fifteenth century, though there is a mention of people holding a similar office but known as 'church-reeves' in 1396. The definition the *Oxford English Dictionary* gives is: 'A lay honorary officer of a parish or district church, elected to assist the incumbent in the discharge of his administrative duties, to manage such various parochial offices as by custom or legislation devolve upon him, and generally to act as the lay representative of the parish in matters of church-organization.'

What it has been historically

It is clear from *Visitation Articles and Injunctions of the Period of the Reformation* (edited by W. H. Frere and W. P. Kennedy and published by the Alcuin Club in 1910) and from *Visitation Articles and Injunctions of the Early Stuart Church* (edited in two volumes by Kenneth Fincham and published by the Church of England Record Society in 1994 and 1998 respectively) that during the sixteenth and seventeenth centuries churchwardens were expected to act as spies and informers, or at the very least as means of control, in the attempt to ensure that reformed principles were being applied in all the parishes of England and Wales. They also had some responsibility for administering the Poor Laws, the original Poor Laws of 1597–8 having provided for the administration of relief to the sick, old people and destitute children through parish overseers who worked with the churchwardens. Judging from the case histories a lot of this work entailed disputes as to which parish had the responsibility for a particular poor person. They would try to establish where a vagrant who had turned up on their doorsteps came from, so that his parish of origin would have to bear the costs of looking after him. Or they would spend time trying to find out who was the 'putative father' of the 'bastard child' of a 'lewd mother', so that he, rather than the parish, could be made to pay for the child's upkeep. The churchwardens and overseers also had the power to require children of the parish to be taken as apprentices, selecting 'for this purpose such children as they shall think their parents are unable to maintain'.[1]

One of the many sets of Articles in Fincham's edition concerns the visitation by Bishop Richard Montague to his diocese of Chichester in 1628, during the course of which the churchwardens and sidesmen were asked questions about religion and doctrine, divine service and administration of the sacraments, the church and its ornaments, sacred utensils and articles, the ministers and preachers of God's word, matrimony, parishioners, schoolmasters, physicians, surgeons (reflecting the Church's responsibility for licensing the medical profession of that time), parish clerks and ecclesiastical officers. These are a few of the Articles of Enquiry (retaining original spellings):

Whether be there any one, or more residing, lodging or abiding in your parish, that holde, defend, set forth, or propose any heresie, errors, or false opinions, contrarie to holy scripture, the three creedes, the booke of thirtie nine articles, the booke of common prayer, the booke of consecrating and ordayning bishopps, priests, and deacons?

Doth your Minister read divine service according to the iniunctions in the booke of common prayer; doth he diminish, alter, exchange the forme prescribed, in part, or in all, using prayers in steede thereof of his own devising, and conceiving?

Have you a font of stone, for the administration of baptisme, set up in the usuall place near the church doore, with a cover to keepe it from dust and soyle?

Doth your Minister alwaies, and at every time, both morning

and evening, reading divine service, and administering the sacraments, and other rites of the Church, ware the surplice according to the canons, and doth he never omitt wearing of the same at such times?

Have any church-wardens retained any of the church goods, and not made a just accompt of what they have received and expended?

(It is hard to imagine that any churchwarden with a sense of self-preservation would have answered 'yes' to that last question – unless, of course, one churchwarden had a grudge against another.) Another bishop, Richard Vaughan, had required that the churchwardens swear their oath during his visitation in 1605, according to the following terms:

You shall sweare, that all affection, favour, hatred, hope of reward or gaine, or feare of displeasure or malice set aside: you shall upon due consideration of the articles given you in charge, present all and everie person, within your parish, as hath committed any offence or fault, or made any default mentioned in these or any of these articles, or which are vehemently suspected or defamed of any such offence, fault or default: wherein you shall deale uprightly and according to truth, neither of malice presenting any contrary to truth, nor of corrupt affection sparing to present any, and so conceal the truth: having in this action God before your eyes, with an earnest zeale to maintaine truth, and to suppresse vice. So helpe you God, and the contents of this booke.

The oath to be taken by churchwardens was simplified in the reign of King Charles II: 'You shall swear, truly and faithfully to execute the office of a churchwarden within your parish, and according to the best of your skill and knowledge present such things and persons as, to your knowledge, are presentable by the laws ecclesiastical of this realm. So help you God, and the contents of this book.' By an act of William IV a declaration that the elected churchwarden would faithfully and diligently perform the duties of the office was substituted for the oath.

The sense of the churchwardens' being expected to act as informers and to sit in judgement on their minister is continued into the nineteenth century. Charles Grevile Prideaux in his *Practical Guide to the Duties of Churchwardens in the Execution of their Office* (which went into sixteen editions between 1841 and 1895) gives a sample list of the sort of Articles regularly asked during the mid-nineteenth century; they were divided into three sections and concerned the minister, the services, the fabric of the building and the life of the parish:

Articles of Inquiry

I

1 Who is your Minister?
2 Does he usually serve his cure himself?
3 Does he reside in the parsonage house?
4 Is he of sober life and conversation?
5 At what hours does he celebrate divine service?
6 Does he read divine service properly habited, reverently, distinctly, and audibly, as prescribed by the Book of Common Prayer, without additions, diminutions, or alterations?
7 Is the sacrament of baptism administered in the church (except in cases of necessity) and during the time of divine service?
8 Are those who are privately baptised, afterwards publicly received into the church?
9 Is the sacrament of the Lord's Supper administered so that every parishioner may receive it thrice a year at the least?
10 Is timely warning given thereof?
11 How often does your Minister preach?
12 Does he publicly instruct and examine the children in the Church Catechism? Where, and at what times?
13 Does he publicly prepare the children for confirmation?
14 Does he visit the sick regularly and diligently?
15 Are your registers deposited in an iron chest; and where is the chest kept?

16 Are the entries duly made, and transcripts sent to the bishop's registry?

II

1 Are the body and roof, tower and steeple, walls and battlements of your church maintained in good repair?

2 Are your windows well glazed and leaded, and are there casements to admit air?

3 Are the floors well paved and even?

4 Is the chancel in good repair?

5 Is your church dry and well aired?

6 Are your pulpit and reading-desk in good order?

7 Have you a large Bible, a Book of Common Prayer for the Minister, and another for the clerk, entire, clean, and in good order?

8 Have you a decent stone font for the administration of baptism, and does it stand in the accustomed place, where fonts have anciently and usually stood, at or near the west end of the church?

9 Have you in your chancel a communion table, with suitable furniture?

10 What several vessels have you for the administration of the Lord's Supper, and of what materials?

11 Are your bells, bell-frames, etc., in thorough repair?

12 Are the doors of your church opened, and the bells rung and tolled, a reasonable time before service?

13 Are the bells rung at other times without the leave of the Minister and one churchwarden?

14 Is your church regularly swept, and kept free from dust and dirt?

15 Is your churchyard well fenced, its doors and gates in good repair, and its churchways well kept up?

16 Are any encroachments made on it? Are any cattle allowed to depasture to the injury of the churchyard and the graves therein?

17 Are the houses and out-houses of your incumbent in good repair?

18 Have you a terrier of all lands, tenements, pensions,

rate-tithes, or portions of tithes, and other dues and customs payable to your incumbent?

III

1 Are your churchwardens chosen every year, according to the custom of your parish, and what is your custom?
2 Are your rates for the repair of your church regularly made, and your accounts passed in vestry?
3 Do you attend divine service regularly, and keep order in the church during its celebration?
4 Do you prevent idle persons from abiding in the church porch, or churchyard, during service?
5 Are there any persons in your parish known or openly suspected of any crime presentable by the ecclesiastical laws of this realm?
6 Are there any who profane the Lord's day by following their worldly callings, or who keep open shops, or suffer persons to tipple in their houses on that day?
7 Is your parish clerk competent to his duties, and of honest life and conversation?
8 Is psalmody duly encouraged under the direction of the Minister?
9 Do you provide bread and wine for the communion, at the charge of your parish?
10 Are there any funds left for the repairs of your church?
11 Is there, or has there been, any free-school, hospital, almshouse, parochial library, or donation to charitable use within your parish?
12 Do you know of any abuse in the management of these charities?
13 Is the key of the church kept where the Minister directs?
14 Are such repairs and improvements made, or in progress, as have been ordered at the last general visitation?
15 Hath any officer of the archdeacon's court demanded or taken undue and unreasonable fees for any cause or matter transacted by him?

The churchwardens' responsibilities for administering the Poor Laws also continued throughout the nineteenth century, though after 1834 the parishes could exercise less individual discretion, a revised and much harsher Poor Law having come into effect in 1834, giving the able-bodied poor the option of either the workhouse or no relief at all.

The standard nineteenth-century legal textbook by Sir Robert Phillimore, revised for a second edition by his son, Sir Walter Phillimore, and entitled *The Ecclesiastical Law of the Church of England* (1895), describes the churchwardens as 'parochial officers for several purposes' and points to their duty to 'inspect the morals and behaviour of the parishioners as well as to take care of the goods and repairs of the church'. Phillimore quotes the great lawyer William Scott Stowell, first Baron Stowell (1745–1836) on churchwardens. Giving judgment in a case Stowell said:

[I]t is proper to consider what are their [the churchwardens'] duties, and I conceive that originally they were confined to the care of the ecclesiastical property of the parish, over which they exercise a discretionary power for specific purposes. In all other respects it is an office of observation and complaint, but not of control, with respect to divine worship; so it is laid down in Ayliffe [*Parergon Juris Canonici Anglicani*, 1726, by John Ayliffe] in one of the best dissertations on the duties of Churchwardens, and in the canons of 1571. In these it is observed that the Churchwardens are appointed to provide the furniture of the church, the bread and wine for the holy sacrament, the surplice and the books necessary for the performance of divine worship, and such as are directed by law; but it is the Minister who has the use. If, indeed, he errs in this respect, it is just matter for complaint, which the Churchwardens are bound to attend to, but the law would not oblige them to complain if they had a power in themselves to redress the abuse. In the service, the Churchwardens have nothing to do but to collect the alms at the offertory; and they may refuse the admission of strange Preachers into the pulpit. For this purpose they are authorised by canon [Canon 50 of 1603], but how? When letters of orders are produced, their authority ceases. Again, if the Minister introduces any irregularity into the service, they have no authority to interfere, but they may complain to the Ordinary of his conduct. I do not say there may not be cases where they may not be bound to interpose; in such cases they may repress, and ought to repress, all indecent interruptions of the service by others, and are the most proper persons to repress them, and they desert their duty if they do not. And if a case should be imagined in which even a preacher himself was guilty of an act grossly offensive either from natural infirmity or from disorderly habits, I will not say that the Churchwardens, and even private persons, might not interpose to preserve the decorum of public worship. But that is a case of instant and overbearing necessity, that supersedes all ordinary rules. In cases which fall short of such a singular pressure, and can wait the remedy of a proper legal complaint, that is the only proper mode to be pursued by a Churchwarden – if private and decent application to the Minister himself shall have failed in preventing what he deems the repetition of an irregularity at all. At the same time it is at his own peril if he makes a public complaint, or even a private complaint, in an offensive manner, of that which is no irregularity at all, and is in truth nothing more than a misrepresentation of his own.

Lord Stowell's words are worthy of serious consideration. Churchwardens had, and continue to have, 'a discretionary power for specific purposes' and, for the most part, this has been exercised by the making of complaints. Stowell was primarily concerned with complaints about irregularities in the conduct of divine worship, and he cautioned the churchwardens to be certain that what they wished to complain about really was an irregularity and that the complaint, whether public or private, was not made in an offensive manner.

In Stowell and Phillimore's day becoming a churchwarden was not necessarily a matter of personal choice; neither was the amount of time they dedicated to the office. Michael Nolan's *Treatise of the Laws for the Relief and Settlement of the Poor* of 1808 includes the following injunction:

The churchwardens and overseers are to meet at least once a month, in the parish church, upon Sunday afternoon, after divine service, to consider of all things concerning their office; and any absenting himself without lawful excuse, or being negligent in their office, or in the execution of the said orders being made, by and with the assent of the justices, or any two of them, shall forfeit for every such default of absence or negligence 20s[hillings].[2]

Lay people, both men and women, resident in the parish might find themselves elected by the Vestry (loosely speaking, the forerunner of the annual meeting) and thus obliged to serve as churchwardens. Those exempt from having to perform this office included peers of the realm, Members of Parliament, the clergy, sheriffs, attorneys of the King's Bench, clerks of the Queen's Bench, apothecaries, medical practitioners, naval officers and Inland Revenue officers. Roman Catholics, Jews, minors, aliens and persons convicted of a felony were all disqualified. A Mr Allnutt sought exemption because he was deaf; his request was refused and Lord Stowell directed him to take the oath and be admitted to the office. Generally a person could not be compelled to serve for a second year, unless this was 'the constant custom of the parish'. In 1767 a Mr Conach had attempted to avoid a second term as churchwarden of St Ethelburga in the City of London (the medieval church almost entirely destroyed by the IRA's Bishopsgate bomb and now largely rebuilt as a centre for reconciliation). It was ruled that, as a second term was the constant custom of the parish, Mr Conach, who had served a year as under-churchwarden, would be compelled to serve a further year as upper-churchwarden.

We no longer have under- and upper-churchwardens, churchwardens today being equal in status and title. We also no longer have vicar's and people's wardens, the origin of these titles being found in the mode of election or appointment before the passing of the Churchwardens Measure 2001. Canon 89 of 1603 said:

All churchwardens or questmen, in every parish, shall be chosen by joint consent of the Minister and parishioners if it may be; but if they cannot agree upon such a choice, then the Minister shall choose one, and the parishioners another: and without such a joint or several choice, none shall take upon them to be churchwardens neither shall they continue any longer than one year in that office, except perhaps they be chosen again in like manner.

There were many customary variations on this practice; hence the question asked at the visitation: 'Are your churchwardens chosen every year, according to the custom of your parish, and what is your custom?' It seemed to be universally the case in the City of London that both churchwardens were appointed by the parishioners alone. Elsewhere in the country a variety of customs prevailed. In Berwick, the minister chose one and the outgoing churchwardens chose the other. At Berkeley in Gloucestershire there were four churchwardens, each elected by a different part of the parish. At Prestwich in Lancashire the outgoing churchwarden presented the rector with the names of two persons and he chose one to be churchwarden for the ensuing year. The parish of St Sepulchre-without-Newgate is partly in the City of London and partly in Middlesex; it had five churchwardens, three for the City and two for the country part of the parish. New parishes, that is to say those created under George III and William IV, were subject to the specific requirement by statute, as follows:

> Two fit and proper persons shall be appointed to act as churchwardens for every church or chapel built or appropriated under the provisions of this act, at the usual period of appointing parish officers in each year, and shall be chosen, one by the incumbent of the church or chapel for the time being, and the other by the inhabitant householders entitled to vote in the election of churchwardens, residing in the district to which the church or chapel shall belong.

The ecclesiastical duties of the churchwardens as listed by Phillimore are very similar to their present duties, but we must always remember that there were no Parochial Church Councils before 1919 but only the Vestry. A Vestry, properly speaking, was, according to Phillimore, 'the assembly of the whole parish met together in some convenient place, for the dispatch of the affairs and business of the parish; and this meeting being commonly holden in the vestry adjoining to, or belonging to the church, it thence took the name of vestry, as the place itself does, from the priest's vestments which are usually deposited and kept there'. The full Vestry meeting could be large and unwieldy, and so select Vestries grew from the practice of appointing a certain number of people each year to manage the affairs of the parish. The select Vestry had no basis in law but again was based on custom, described by Phillimore as 'constant immemorial usage'.

One might have expected the experiences of churchwardens from the nineteenth century and earlier to have left us a legacy of stories and humour, but such is not the case (perhaps they were kept too busy drawing up complaints, and the clergy defending themselves, for either side to have much time for levity). Nevertheless, Harry Saxon does have some tales to tell in his *Churchwardens of the Past*, published in 1908, and here are two of them. The first is a reminder that it is the duty of the church-wardens to arrange for the collection to be gathered from the congregation; the second is a warning against pomposity:

> During the collection for church expenses, the junior church-warden pushed his plate about manfully and with great persis-tency, with running comments and remarks such as the following:
>
> 'And thank you, sir.'
> And when a larger piece of silver was put in would add:
> 'And thank you, sir, very kindly.'
> And when a piece of gold was put in there would be added:
> 'And we are much obliged to you, sir, indeed.'

This same churchwarden strongly resisted the replacement of plates by bags because it made it impossible to see what was being put in.

The second story sounds rather like something that could happen at a church in the City of London:

> There was a churchwarden I knew in the great Metropolis years ago, who was punctilious and somewhat pedantic in the discharge of his duties at all church functions, especially when his lordship the Right Reverend Father in God, the Bishop of the diocese, was *en evidence* in the Parish Church.

To see him process his lordship up into the pulpit from the altar steps was a treat.

First he himself walked in the procession, as if he was on hot bricks. Next his great care was that his lordship should not immolate himself in canonical vestments upon the floor of the church during the time his lordship was under his verger care. To guard against such a possibility the churchwarden as the pilot engine to his lordship, after noting any 'impediments' in the way, such as hassocks and stray books, &c, would carefully hustle the same out of the pathway of the bishop.

But, alas, in his care for the safe passageway of his lordship, he neglected something pertaining to the safety of his own, and himself came a heavy fall on one occasion over a stray thin cloth kneeler that had got under his feet, and down he came full sprawl, snapping his wand of office in twain at the same time.

It was a pitiable sight somewhat to see the churchwarden picking up the broken pieces of his wand and rubbing his broken shins as his lordship swept by, apparently unmoved by the fiasco that had overtaken the obsequiously polite and worthy member of the faithful laity in his discharge of his duties as churchwarden on the occasion.

How it has changed and developed, and what it should – or could – be now

Parochial Church Councils (PCCs) were established by the Enabling Act 1919 and came into existence in July 1921. The Councils took on most of the powers, duties and liabilities from the parish Vestry, except with regard to the election of churchwardens and sidesmen and some other matters. They also took on the powers, duties and liabilities of the churchwardens of the parish with regard to the financial affairs of the church and the keeping of accounts, the care, maintenance, preservation and insurance of the fabric of the church and of its goods and ornaments, and the care and maintenance of any churchyard. None of these powers, however, affected 'the property of the churchwardens in the goods and ornaments of the church or their powers duties and liabilities with respect to visitations'. It is because of these changes, as well as the abolition of certain civic duties of churchwardens, that old books on the duties of churchwardens make very little sense to the contemporary holders of the office.

Though Vestries in the traditional sense passed out of existence with the creation of PCCs, they retained a role in relation to the choosing of churchwardens until the Churchwardens (Appointments and Resignation) Measure 1964. Even in the late 1990s, however, it was possible to see notices announcing the annual Vestry meeting. This simply shows how long it can take to change procedures in the Church, even when new measures are put in place. The 1964 Measure allowed for adherence to 'existing custom', defined as a custom that had been in existence for at least 40 years prior to the date of the commencement of the Measure (27 February 1964). Such customs were considered as special in each case and there was a requirement that they should be clearly proven.

The most recent stage in the development of legislation regarding the office of churchwarden is the Churchwardens Measure 2001. This Measure has a history which itself reflects the nature of the office. In December 1993 the Policy Committee of the General Synod decided to set up a working party 'to review the law relating to the appointment and tenure of lay office-holders in the parish and to bring forward draft legislation'. The working party was chaired by Dr Christina Baxter, Principal of St John's College, Nottingham, and a member of the General Synod. Behind the Policy Committee's decision was a series of problems concerning the lay office-holders, and specifically churchwardens, which in some instances had led to serious pastoral difficulties.

That conflicts can arise between churchwardens and ministers is hardly surprising given the history of the office, with its apparent onus on the churchwardens to report any irregularities on the part of their minister. Some people may even be attracted to the office, consciously or unconsciously, by a desire to oppose the minister and to have the power to do so effectively. Clearly this is not a good reason for seeking the office. Ian Russell wrote in *The Churchwarden's Handbook*:

As far as a potential churchwarden is concerned, if there is an unwillingness even to attempt to co-operate then their motive for agreeing to nomination must be in question. It cannot be right for someone to be chosen as churchwarden whose aim in their period of office is to thwart the minister in his or her ministry.[3]

The report of the working party set up by the Policy Committee of the General Synod devoted 76 of its 123 paragraphs to church-wardens. A summary of its findings and recommendations will help us to see the main issues involved. (We have used the same headings as those employed in the report.)

A. Number of churchwardens

Two churchwardens was the rule in the 1964 Measure except in parishes with a long-standing custom providing for some other number. The working party supported the general principle that 'each parish is responsible for providing two people to serve as churchwardens'. The 2001 Measure says 'there shall be two churchwardens of every parish' though it tucks away in a later paragraph the crucial words, 'in the case of any parish where there is an existing custom which regulates the number of churchwar-dens ... nothing in this Measure shall affect that custom'. The working party was not concerned about the occasional parish with three, four or even more churchwardens, but rather with the parish where it is possible to find only one churchwarden. Here they favoured a discretionary power to be exercised by the bishop to allow, for one year at a time, the appointment of just one churchwarden. The working party also discussed the rather rare situation where no one was willing to serve. This actually fell outside their remit because, if it were permitted by a similar discre-tionary power, it would also be necessary to make provision for vesting in some other person or body the churchwarden's rights, powers and duties, together with their ownership of the movable goods of the church.

B. Eligibility for appointment

Most of the points made by the working party have been included in the 2001 Measure, and particularly those regulations that deal with disqualifications. There are, however, four illuminating areas of discussion that did not lead directly to legislation. The first concerned maximum age and fixed maximum period of service. The 2001 Measure introduced a provision that, without special resolution, a churchwarden was not eligible for immediate re-election after six terms in office, but the discussion was concerned with two difficult situations. One was the problem of age, when with advancing years a churchwarden is not as effective as he or she used to be, but is not aware of it and would find it hurtful if other parishioners advocated retirement. The other was caused by a prolonged period in office such that the churchwarden lost his or her original drive and enthusiasm and where other likely candidates were reluctant to stand for fear of causing offence or creating dissension by opposing a churchwarden of long standing. Problems of this sort cannot be resolved by legislation, and it should be remembered that for every parish that has problems with an elderly, very long-serving churchwarden, there are ten that are deeply grateful for the experience, wisdom and devoted service given by churchwardens who have long passed secular retirement ages. The thrust of our argument in this book is that churchwardens should be realistic about their ability to discharge their duties and be ready to step aside if necessary; they should also be ready to return to the office on another occasion when the parish needs their skills and experience.

The second area of discussion concerned divorced people. Among the submissions made to the working party was one that a churchwarden who was divorced while holding office should be automatically removed from office. The members held that, as it was possible for a person to be divorced against his or her will without being guilty of any misconduct, and as divorce and even remarriage were not necessarily bars to ordination, any such move was inappropriate, as was any suggestion that divorced people generally should be ineligible for election as churchwardens. It is for the parishioners to decide whether or not a person is a suitable candidate.

The third area concerned the spouses of the clergy. One submission argued that they should not be permitted to hold the office of churchwarden. The working party accepted that 'allowing the incumbent's spouse to be a churchwarden could occasionally give rise to difficulties and strained relations within the parish and could exclude someone else from office who would otherwise have been willing to stand', but again it was not felt appropriate to legislate on the matter. Our own view is that it is inappropriate for clergy spouses to be churchwardens or PCC members in the parish served by their husband or wife because it is very difficult for people to speak openly on difficult matters in such circumstances.

The fourth area concerned the clergy as churchwardens. The working party was advised that there was no legal rule disqualifying a member of the clergy from holding office as a churchwarden, amazing as that seems. Again the working party recognized the possibility of exceptional circumstances in which a retired cleric or perhaps a non-stipendiary minister would be the only suitable person, but still felt it inappropriate that a cleric should fulfil the role of one who was to be 'foremost in representing the laity'. The revised qualification rules require a churchwarden to be on the church electoral roll and, since only lay people can be on the roll, the clergy are not eligible for election as churchwardens.

C. Period of office and time and manner of choice of churchwardens

The 1964 Measure held to the idea that the churchwardens were appointed rather than elected, and that by the joint consent of the minister and the meeting, but the members of the working party were aware that the procedure was simply not being followed. In many parishes the minister automatically chose one churchwarden, and the meeting elected the other, without any effort being made to arrive at joint consent. The method adopted by many incumbents was that of ascertaining in advance whether the existing churchwardens were willing to serve another year and, if they did, offering them to the meeting for agreement. This normally worked well and certainly met the requirement for joint consent. The working party was concerned that when there was disagreement it was unclear how to carry out an election. In fact the rules for an election were found in the Church Representation Rules and not in the Churchwardens Measure.

In these circumstances [the working party reported] a strong-minded minister may decide on a procedure which everyone present accepts (whether or not it is within the terms of the Measure), but unless that happens confusion arises, people leave the meeting feeling doubtful about whether the legal requirements have been satisfied, and the result is dissension and strained relations within the parish or even the beginning of pastoral breakdown. Indeed, in the increasingly litigious age in which we live, such cases could well give rise to legal proceedings in the secular courts at some time in the future.

The working party was certain that the Church of England had to have a clear and easily understandable procedure for the choice of churchwardens and this is what led to the election procedure set down in the 2001 Measure. They recognized the need for the minister to have at least one churchwarden with whom he or she had a good working relationship and it was this concern that led to the rather odd procedure of objecting to a candidate. The working party wanted nominations to be submitted two clear days before the meeting, to allow adequate time for reflection, but the 2001 Measure stated only that nominations must be received by the minister before the commencement of the meeting (whereas nominations for PCC membership can be made during the meeting).

D. Existing customs

The working party noted the existence of customs and considered them to be anomalies that did not give rise to substantial problems. Paragraph 12 of the 2001 Measure does, however, allow for the abolition of existing customs by resolution of the meeting of parishioners.

E. Admission to office

The working party held that the admission to office was an important part of the process by which a person became a churchwarden and set out to strengthen the regulations about it. They also saw the annual visitation as an essential feature of the churchwardens' relation to the bishop and archdeacon. After examining various forms for visitations, they recommended that a standardized pattern should not be imposed but that the visitation should include

- the making of the declaration that the person will faithfully and diligently perform the duties of the office;
- the formal admission to office;
- the archdeacon's charge;
- an act of worship;
- an opportunity to meet and talk with other churchwardens;
- an opportunity for personal contact with the archdeacon and, if possible, with the diocesan registrar.

F. Tenure of office

It was this section of the report, and the draft Measure that followed from it, that gave rise to the greatest concern, with the result that the main recommendations, about removal from office and suspension, were not included in the 2001 Measure. The working party's recommendations on resignation and automatic vacation of office have passed into law, and, if a churchwarden who was not disqualified at the time of election is subsequently disqualified (and so unable to be re-elected), he or she can no longer continue to serve and the office is vacated.

There was, and still is, no procedure for the removal of a churchwarden from office, other than that in the Incumbents (Vacation of Benefices) Measure 1977. From the submissions they received the working party identified three types of case where such a procedure was, in their view, necessary:

1 where the churchwarden ceases to be able to fulfil his or her duties, for example because of illness or absence from the parish, but refuses to resign (or possibly, in the case of serious illness, is unable to do so);
2 where the churchwarden is guilty, or accused, of a serious breach of his or her legal duties, for example by refusing to co-operate with the incumbent or stirring up dissension in the parish;
3 where the churchwarden commits, or is accused of, other serious misconduct, so that his or her continuing to act as

churchwarden would result in grave scandal and would be seriously detrimental to the Church, either in the parish or more widely.

The working party accepted that these situations did not arise frequently, but when they did they invariably had a serious adverse effect on church life. It might be thought that the system of annual elections would mean that the parishioners could simply elect someone else but the meeting often has a degree of sympathy for the churchwarden and re-elects him or her. The working party proposed legislation that would give the bishop express powers to deal with such situations and that these should be the power to suspend and the power to remove from office. Hard cases do not make good law and the legislation had to be phrased in a way that gave the bishop maximum room for manoeuvre. The draft Measure said that 'the bishop may for any cause which appears to him to be good and reasonable' suspend a churchwarden from office or remove him or her. When a person was removed from office, the bishop could also 'disqualify that person from being a churchwarden or member or officer of the parochial church council of the parish in question and of such other parishes in his diocese as he may specify during such period as he may specify'. These powers and the related procedures for appeal passed through the General Synod but did not find favour with Parliament and were not included in the 2001 Measure.

This issue will almost certainly be revisited at some future date, and the basis of suspension or removal will need to be specified more clearly than some 'cause' that seems 'good and reasonable' to the bishop. Local authorities are now required to produce codes of conduct for members and a violation of the code leads to disciplinary action. If a similar procedure is followed for churchwardens and Parochial Church Councils, then an office-holder could be suspended or removed from office but only because of a proven breach of the code. The provisions of the draft Measure gave the bishop too much power with regard to officers who had been duly elected and admitted to office by proper process. It is likely that the procedure as set down would also have led to possible violation of European human-rights legislation.

G. Deputy churchwardens

The only legally recognized deputies are those elected in a parish with two or more places of worship (as allowed by Rule 18 of the Church Representation Rules 2006) and in team ministries (under Schedule 3 to the Pastoral Measure 1983). The working party received a number of submissions arguing for the appointment of other deputies but decided against introducing any new legislation to allow for this.

H. Guild churches in the City of London

Guild churches exist only in the City of London. They were created by an Act of Parliament in 1952 which attempted to rationalize the parochial system in the City by keeping some parish churches, with geographical parishes, and making others non-parochial (and calling them 'guild churches'). The parish of St Bartholomew the Great is a parish church (since 1539) that had a very small geographical parish before annexing the adjoining parish of St Botolph, Aldersgate, when it became a guild church. The legislation concerning guild churches differs in a number of ways from that which affects parish churches and, because the guild-church system was under review, the working party decided not to include them in the proposed Measure (see para. 9).

I. Channel Islands, Isle of Man and Diocese in Europe

This section is a reminder that the Church of England regulations may have to be interpreted differently in different places and may not come into operation automatically. It is also worth recalling that, since its disestablishment by the Welsh Church Act 1914, the Anglican Church in Wales is governed quite independently of the Church of England and that the office of churchwarden is regulated by the appropriate provisions in the Constitution of the Church in Wales.

J. Special powers of the bishop

These were provided for in Section 11 of the 1964 Measure and are contained in Section 10 of the 2001 Measure.

This is the background to the position of churchwardens, who are no longer overseers of the poor of the parish, but continue to have quite specific and significant responsibilities with regard to the church.

The churchwarden in the twenty-first century needs somehow to combine a knowledge and understanding of the history of the office and its time-honoured roles with a greater degree of co-operation and collaboration than was possible in the more hierarchical days of the Church's past. We have moved on from the days when departure from Reformation practices could be seen as an act of treason and, though changes wrought by a new incumbent on the traditions of a particular church can still make feelings run high and blood boil, the effective churchwarden knows he or she can accomplish far more by sympathetic persuasion and timely advice than by churning out innumerable complaints and firing them off to the archdeacon or the bishop. But there is no denying that the contemporary churchwarden's role requires a very delicate balancing act, as the office has three distinct aspects:

- the churchwardens of a parish are officers of the bishop;
- the churchwardens are the parish priest's principal collaborators;
- the churchwardens are the principal representatives of the laity on the Parochial Church Council.

These three aspects do not always sit easily together and there may be some conflict between them. The struggle to resolve such conflict, to find the right balance, is not unusual in the Church; similar conflicts are apparent in the need of the parish priest to balance the calls of the parish and the wider Church, the need for study and the requirements of pastoral care, administration and liturgical preparation. Likewise, churchwardens can find themselves being pulled in many different directions with very little to help them decide what is the right course of action.

Perhaps no one has better or more inspiringly expressed the

requirement for churchwardens to achieve the right balance between the needs of incumbent and PCC than W. S. Wigglesworth, registrar of the diocese of Derby during the 1940s. In 'The Office of Churchwarden', the chapter he contributed to his bishop's (A. E. J. Rawlinson's) volume entitled *The World's Question and the Christian Answer*, he rehearsed the churchwardens' responsibilities as guardians of both the church and its contents and, in some sense, of the moral character and public decency of the parish, and then went on to say:

> What is the constant duty of the Churchwardens in this connection is to assist the Incumbent in his work in the parish. It is to the Incumbent that the care of souls is committed, and the part played by the Churchwardens and the PCC must of necessity be secondary to the Incumbent's. Churchwardens, however, have this great advantage over the PCC: the Council is a corporation, but they are human beings; they are therefore in a better position to represent the Incumbent to the parishioners and the parishioners to the Incumbent. Let it be their task therefore to see that each understands the other, that there is peace in the parish, that things temporal are so arranged that all may be well with things spiritual.[4]

The churchwarden shares in the ministry that Christ has entrusted to his Church. In his 2001 visitation charge the Archdeacon of London, the Venerable Peter Delaney, described churchwardens as 'the leading lay people in the parish', who 'must be seen to be setting an example in ministry, in worship, and in seeking to witness to their Lord and Saviour'. He drew the attention of clergy and churchwardens to the Letter of the Apostle Paul to the Philippians (2.1–11):

> If then there is any encouragement in Christ, any consolation from love, any sharing in the Spirit, any compassion and sympathy, make my joy complete: be of the same mind, having the same love, being in full accord and of one mind. Do nothing from selfish ambition or conceit, but in humility regard others as better than yourselves. Let each of you look not to your own interests, but to the interests of others. Let the same mind be in

you that was in Christ Jesus, who, though he was in the form of God, did not regard equality with God as something to be exploited, but emptied himself, taking the form of a slave, being born in human likeness. And being found in human form, he humbled himself and became obedient to the point of death – even death on a cross. Therefore God also highly exalted him and gave him the name that is above every name, so that at the name of Jesus every knee should bend, in heaven and on earth and under the earth, and every tongue should confess that Jesus Christ is Lord, to the glory of God the Father.[5]

St Paul was addressing the young church at Philippi and reminding the Christians there, in a commercial world and a trading city, that they must have regard to the attitude they show one another and that the manner in which they behave demonstrates the nature of their commitment to Christ. He also makes it clear that Christian communities are built not by arrogance and pride but by humility and service, and so charges them to have the same mind that was in Christ Jesus. Archdeacon Delaney went on to address the specific role of churchwardens:

To share leadership within the Church of God is a privilege; but it is a privilege firmly based upon the Jesus of the Gospels. It is leadership described in the Letter to those Christians at Philippi. It looks like Jesus Christ himself. And what did he look like? Like a figure hanging on a cross with nails in his hands and feet and wearing a crown of thorns. Those are the marks of church-wardens, nails and thorns and a wooden cross. These describe the ministry and mission of a Warden. These should also be the marks of your clergy and congregations, no cross, no crown. If the centre of our lives is where Jesus is, the rest will follow.

What should occupy the Wardens, people and clergy of the city parishes is a strategy of mission, a teaching plan for the faith, worship provided in such a way that it is evangelistic as well as transcendent.

The Archdeacon also reminded the churchwardens that it was not an 'us and them' situation, with 'us' being the parishes, and 'them' the diocese:

It is to enable church communities to grow and develop that a diocese exists. To provide a framework for extending the work of Christ to free Christian men and women, that is why we have in place Chancellors, Registrars, Archdeacons, Area Deans, Lay Chairmen, Wardens and PCCs. We are all in it together. When it does not work together as a whole the Body of Christ is torn apart.

Archdeacons across the Church of England and in other parts of the Anglican Communion would doubtless say the same or similar things when addressing churchwardens and it is essential, before one goes on to look at the specific roles of the churchwardens, and before one aspires to the office, to see this bigger picture.

Nearly 120 years ago Archbishop Edward White Benson addressed remarks to the clergy and laity of his diocese of Canterbury during his visitation. He based his addresses on the gifts of the Spirit: wisdom, understanding, counsel, strength, knowledge, godliness and holy fear. Speaking of churchwardens, he had this to say:

> Most grateful am I for the courage, the earnestness and the dili-
> gence which is frankly and fully placed at the service of our
> parishes – and I will add for the loyal kindness with which diffi-
> cult cases are treated. Priests and people find in their church-
> wardens the best of helpers. The office is worthy of all honour,
> and the general discharge of it is worthy of the office.

♦ 2 ♦

How people become churchwardens

Qualifications

In order to be eligible for election to the office of churchwarden you must fulfil all of the following criteria:

1 Your name must appear on the church electoral roll of the parish where you are going to stand.
2 You must be an actual communicant.
3 You must be 21 years of age or older.
4 You must not be disqualified under various pieces of legislation (see below).
5 You must not have already served as churchwarden of the same parish for six successive periods of office since the passing of the Churchwardens Measure 2001 (No. 1).

Each of these criteria is dealt with in turn.

1 Electoral roll
To be on the church electoral roll (not to be confused with the local-government register of electors, which is used for local and parliamentary elections) you need to have filled in a form. The electoral roll is normally revised every sixth year, the last revision having taken place in 2007, and everyone wishing to be on the roll has to complete a new form at each revision. The form involves a declaration that a person is baptized, is over 16 years of age, and falls into one of the following categories:

• is a member of the Church of England or of a church in communion with it (i.e. another Anglican/Episcopalian church and certain other churches, but not on the whole other English denominations, such as Roman Catholic, Baptist, Methodist or Presbyterian) and is resident in the parish; or

- is a member of the Church of England or of a church in communion with it and is not resident in the parish, but has habitually attended public worship there during the previous six months; or
- is a member in good standing of some other non-Anglican church that 'subscribes to the doctrine of the Holy Trinity' and who for these purposes also declares himself or herself to be a member of the Church of England after attending public worship habitually in the parish during the previous six months.

This third category was created specifically to deal with rural communities. In the parish of Weston (Dr Dudley's first parish), a village in North Hertfordshire, the Methodist chapel had been closed for several years. Most of those villagers who were Methodists belonged to Letchworth Methodist Church but also worshipped at the parish church and were involved in its life. Until this category was added they were not able to vote in PCC elections or stand for election themselves, and this provision allowed them to do so. The significant words are 'in good standing'. This category is not intended, for example, as a way of allowing lapsed or excommunicate Roman Catholics to declare themselves to be Church of England without any further formalities, but it does mean that a member of a non-Anglican church can be entered on the electoral roll and, if actually communicant, can become a churchwarden.

A person, if qualified, may be on the electoral roll of a number of parishes but, if wishing to stand for office, must choose one parish in which to do so. A person cannot be a churchwarden in two parishes unless they form what is described as 'related parishes'. According to Section 1(5) of the Churchwardens Measure 2001, a related parish means a parish

- belonging to the benefice to which the first-mentioned parish belongs; or
- belonging to a benefice held in plurality with the benefice to which the first-mentioned parish belongs; or
- having the same minister as the first-mentioned parish.

To understand this you have to grasp that a benefice may contain more than one parish, that a priest may hold two benefices in plurality, and that a priest may minister to several parishes as priest-in-charge or as vicar of one and priest-in-charge of another without those parishes forming a benefice. In the late 1980s, for example, the vicar of Weston was also priest-in-charge of Ardeley. Under these provisions a person on the electoral rolls of each of the parishes could have been elected (in separate parochial elections) as churchwarden of each, but was permitted to do this only because one person served as minister of both parishes, there being no formal or legal union between them.

Note that you must be a lay person to be on the electoral roll of any church; clergy are ineligible.

2 Actually communicant

An 'actual communicant' originally meant someone who receives Communion in the parish at least at Christmas, Easter and Whitsun. It is no longer the case that it must be in the parish or on these particular festivals. In the Church of England it is necessary to be both baptized and confirmed before becoming a communicant. This requirement does not apply in certain other Anglican or Episcopalian churches. In the American Episcopal Church, for example, it is sufficient to be baptized.

The Churchwardens Measure uses two different definitions, the one being a revision of the other. In the specific instance of the election of churchwardens of the guild churches in the City of London, it defines 'actual communicant member of the Church of England' as 'a member of the Church of England who is confirmed or ready and desirous of being confirmed and has received Communion according to the use of the Church of England or a church in communion with the Church of England at least three times during the twelve months preceding the date of his election or appointment'.[6] Elsewhere the revised definition is given, the one that is also found in the Church Representation Rules 2006 (Rule 54):

'[A]ctual communicant' means a person who has received communion according to the use of the Church of England or a church in communion with the Church of England at least three times during the twelve months preceding the date of his election or appointment being a person whose name is on the roll of a parish and is either

(a) confirmed or ready and desirous of being confirmed; or
(b) receiving the Holy Communion in accordance with the provisions of Canon B15A paragraph 1(b).

This latter reference is to the permission to admit to the Holy Communion 'baptised persons who are communicant members of other Churches which subscribe to the doctrine of the Holy Trinity, and who are in good standing in their own Church' – in other words, the same people who may be entered on the electoral roll of a parish in the third category.

3 Twenty-one years of age or older
This needs no explanation.

4 Disqualification under various pieces of legislation
A person is disqualified from standing for election to the office of churchwarden if he or she

- is disqualified from being a charity trustee under Section 72(1) of the Charities Act 1993 (c. 10);
- has been convicted of any offence mentioned in Schedule 1 to the Children and Young Persons Act 1933 (c. 12);
- is disqualified under Section 10(6) of the Incumbents (Vacation of Benefices) Measure 1977 (No. 1).

This third disqualification is an interesting one; it comes from the part of the Measure that concerns the breakdown of a pastoral relationship. When there is a serious breakdown in the pastoral relationship between an incumbent and the parishioners a request may be made to the bishop, by the incumbent, the archdeacon or a two-thirds majority of the lay members of the PCC, asking for an enquiry. First, the archdeacon is asked to report (unless the archdeacon is the incumbent or the person making the request) and then, if recommended, an enquiry is made by a provincial tribunal. The procedure is set down in the Measure, and only one possible finding of the tribunal concerns us here. If the tribunal finds that there is a serious breakdown to which the conduct of the incumbent has contributed over a substantial period *and* that the conduct of the parishioners over a substantial period has also contributed to it, then the bishop may rebuke such of the parishioners as he thinks fit and 'may, if he thinks fit, disqualify such of them as he thinks fit from being a churchwarden or officer of the parochial church council of the parish in question and of such other parishes in his diocese as he may specify during such period not exceeding five years as he may specify'.

5 Successive periods of office

This final cause of disqualification, preventing anyone from serving as churchwarden of the same parish for more than six successive periods of office, is a new provision which took effect from the elections in 2002. Each period of office is of one year's duration and runs from annual meeting to annual meeting. Thus a person who, in 2008, had been churchwarden of the same parish for six terms would be disqualified for two years, i.e. 'until the annual meeting of the parishioners to elect churchwardens in the next year but one' (Section 3 of the Churchwardens Measure 2001). This new provision is easily set aside, however. Section 3 also states that 'a meeting of parishioners may by resolution decide that this section shall not apply in relation to the parish concerned. Any such resolution may be revoked by a subsequent meeting of the parishioners.'

CHECKLIST

Qualifications for a churchwarden
You are qualified if you are

- a lay person
- at least 21 years of age
- an actual communicant
- on the electoral roll
- not disqualified in any other way.

It can happen that, for good reason, a parish wishes to elect a churchwarden who is not qualified under the second, third or fourth of the points in the checklist. If the circumstances are exceptional, the bishop may permit a person who does not meet all these requirements to hold the office, but the permission applies to only one period in office and will need to be renewed if the exceptional circumstances continue.

Process of election

Churchwardens have to be elected every year no later than 30 April. The electors are the parishioners gathered at a meeting convened by the minister, using a notice affixed on or near the principal door of the parish church and any other place of worship in the parish for at least two Sundays before the meeting, specifying the place, day and time of the meeting, and signed by the minister. If there is no minister or the minister cannot or will not do it, the notice is displayed by and signed by a churchwarden.

Those eligible to attend are (a) the minister, (b) those whose names are on the church electoral roll of the parish, and (c) those who are resident in the parish and whose names are entered on the local-government register of electors by virtue of being resident. To check the eligibility of those present it would be necessary to have a copy of the electoral roll and of the local-government register. Copies of the latter are available, for a fee, from the local-authority offices. Unfortunately civil parish, ward and constituency boundaries are quite different from ecclesiastical parish boundaries and it will take quite a lot of work to check eligibility. It could be important in the event of a disputed election.

The minister takes the chair or, if the minister is absent, the meeting elects a chairman. The meeting of parishioners has the power to determine its own rules of procedure and to adjourn (though the election must still be made by 30 April). While procedures are being sorted out, a question – as to whether to adjourn, for example, or whether to decide that the disqualification after six successive terms does or does not apply – may be put to the meeting. If there is an equal division of votes on the question, the chairman shall not have a casting vote, and the motion on that question shall be treated as lost. A person appointed by the meeting acts as clerk of the meeting and records the minutes. The procedure for nomination is set down in the Churchwardens Measure 2001 and that for conducting the election is set down in the Church Representation Rules 2006 (Rule 11) with some slight variations.

Candidates for election as churchwardens must be nominated and seconded by persons eligible to attend the meeting and the nomination paper must include a statement, signed by the person nominated, to the effect that he or she is willing to serve as church-warden and is not disqualified. No specific form is given for this, but that in Example 2.1 would do.

EXAMPLE 2.1 Nomination of candidate for the office of churchwarden

We, the undersigned, being eligible to attend the meeting for the election of churchwardens in this parish of _____, nominate _____ for the office of churchwarden of this parish for the year _____.
Nominator: _____
Seconder: _____

Statement by candidate
I, _____, am willing to serve, if elected, as churchwarden of the parish of _____ for the year _____.
I am 21 years of age or older, an actual communicant, and my name appears on the electoral roll of this parish.
I am not disqualified from such office under Section 2(1), (2) or (3) of the Churchwardens Measure 2001 (No. 1).
Signed: _____
Date: _____

The nomination paper must be received by the minister of the parish (or the churchwarden who convened the meeting) before the commencement of the meeting. If the candidate is not qualified (by being 21 or over, an actual communicant, and on the electoral roll), and if application has been made to the bishop because of exceptional circumstances, the bishop's permission must be given before the nomination paper is received by the minister.

If there are more candidates nominated than positions available, there shall be an election. A clerk in holy orders, if resident in the parish and on the local-government register of electors, is entitled to vote; this entitlement does not extend, however, to the minister of the parish. Each person entitled to vote shall have as many votes as there are vacancies but may not give more than one vote to any one candidate. Votes may be given by show of hands unless one or more persons object, in which case they may either be given on voting papers 'signed by the voter on the reverse thereof' or, if requested by at least 10 per cent of the people present and voting, on numbered voting papers. This third option is a way of avoiding something so clearly opposed to the principle of a secret ballot as signing one's name on the back of the voting paper (presumably intended as a means of preventing unqualified voting). Where numbered voting papers are used, a record should be made of the identity of each person who has been given one, but the record 'so long as it is retained' must be kept separate from the voting papers. (The Church Representation Rules do not, however, specify how long such records should be retained.)

Where an equal number of votes is cast so that the election cannot be decided, then the decision shall be made by lot (by placing the names in a hat, for example, and drawing one out, or by asking the candidates to 'draw the short straw'). There is of course a biblical precedent for making such a decision by lot; in the first chapter of the Acts of the Apostles we read:

> Having nominated two candidates, Joseph known as Barsabbas, whose surname was Justus, and Matthias, they prayed, 'Lord, you can read everyone's heart; show us therefore which of these two you have chosen to take over this ministry and apostolate, which Judas abandoned to go to his proper place'. They then drew lots for them, and as the lot fell to Matthias, he was listed as one of the twelve apostles.[7]

Here is a summary of the procedure using the option of numbered voting papers:

1 issue numbered ballot papers to qualified voters (who should be the only people present), making a record on a separate sheet of who has been given which number;

2 give the record of numbers and names to the presiding officer, to be kept separately from the completed ballot papers;

3 ask the tellers to collect the papers;

4 ask if there are any more papers and then declare the ballot closed;

5 allow the tellers to count (perhaps at a table in full view of the meeting);

6 receive the count and declare the result;

7 if the vote is tied, decide by lot.

The Churchwardens Measure contains one further significant provision (Section 4[5]):

> If it appears to the Minister of the parish that the election of any particular person nominated might give rise to serious difficulties between the Minister and that person in the carrying out of their respective functions the Minister may, before the election is conducted, make a statement to the effect that only one churchwarden is to be elected by the meeting. In that event one churchwarden shall be appointed by the Minister from among the persons nominated, the name of the person so appointed being announced before the election is conducted, and the other shall then be elected by the meeting.

This curious provision, which seems to hark back to Canon 89 of 1603 (quoted on pp. 9–10 above) sets out a problem but does nothing to resolve it. Imagine that, in a given parish, two churchwardens are to be elected. *A, B, C* and *D* are duly nominated. *C* is a person who has hitherto opposed the minister on every matter and they particularly disagree on worship – the minister favours *Common Worship* and *C* is utterly devoted to the Prayer Book. The minister invokes the provisions of the Measure and states that only one churchwarden will be elected by the meeting. The minister then announces that he or she has appointed *A*. The meeting votes for the other churchwarden and elects C! The serious difficulties remain.

The result of the election is to be announced as soon as possible and a notice of the result is to be displayed, for not less than 14 days, in the same manner as the notice convening the meeting.

Admission to office

Though elected by 30 April, the new churchwardens cannot take up office until they have been admitted by the bishop or his 'substitute duly appointed'. At the time of admission they promise that they will faithfully and diligently perform the duties of the office and subscribe a declaration to that effect, together with one stating that they are not disqualified under Section 2(1), (2) or (3) of the Measure (i.e. the same declaration that was made on the nomination paper). Admission to office has to take place by 31 July.

Churchwardens coming in or going out of office form three types:

- an existing churchwarden who is re-elected;
- an existing churchwarden who is not re-elected;
- a newly elected churchwarden.

The original term of office of an existing churchwarden who is re-elected ends when he or she is admitted to the next term of office (before 31 July), but if the churchwarden somehow does not get around to being admitted again, then the original term of office ends on 31 July. It is a bit confusing, so it might be worth giving some names and dates for the election of churchwardens in two parishes (see Example 2.2). There could be another version of this rather complicated scenario, as in Example 2.3.

EXAMPLE 2.2

James Smith and Mary Brown were elected as churchwardens in April 2003. James had been churchwarden already. Mary had not been churchwarden before, but was elected to succeed Henry Robinson. Mary went to be admitted on 28 June, so Henry's term of office ended that day. James was admitted on the same day and so he started his second term.

In the next-door parish Douglas Jones and Susan Ward were elected. Douglas had been churchwarden before and Susan had not, but succeeded Michael Gray. Susan went to be admitted on 28 June, and so Michael's term ended on that day. Douglas was away on business and did not get admitted. 31 July passed and his original term of office expired. As he had not been admitted for his next term, a casual vacancy was deemed to have arisen.

EXAMPLE 2.3

Philip Hall and Alice North are the existing churchwardens. Neither of them is re-elected. John Bourne and David Harris are elected. John goes to be admitted on 28 June. David will go later. Which of the existing wardens, Philip and Alice, ends their period of office on 28 June? The Measure says that 'where there is doubt as to which of the new churchwardens is that person's successor in office the bishop may designate one of the new churchwardens as that person's successor' for these purposes.

Why does it matter? Primarily because of the responsibilities that the churchwardens have for the church's movable property and because they are *ex officio* members of the PCC. A person appointed or elected as churchwarden becomes a member of the PCC immediately and this period continues until admission to office or 31 July. If the newly elected churchwarden has not been admitted by then, a casual vacancy is declared and the right to be on the PCC lapses. There could just be a crucial issue at the PCC that is decided by a single vote; then the question is: which outgoing churchwarden had a right to vote? The provisions of the Measure provide the solution, though the answer will involve the already heavily burdened bishop.

The Churchwardens Measure 2001 does not give any specific wording for the declaration to be made, and signed, by churchwardens when they are admitted to office. This is the form used in the diocese of London:

> We, being churchwardens duly elected to serve for the year _____, do solemnly and sincerely declare that we will faithfully and diligently perform the duties of our said office in the church in which we have been elected to serve, and that we will, to the best of our knowledge, seek to represent the lay members of the church and to co-operate with our incumbent. We will endeavour, by word and example, to encourage the church members in the practice of true religion. We will seek to promote unity and peace among them, and will present such persons and things as are presentable by the Laws Ecclesiastical of this Realm.

The bishop or duly appointed substitute, usually the archdeacon, says: 'As Bishop (Archdeacon, etc.) of _____, I admit you and each of you to your respective offices as churchwardens. And may the Lord defend you, and prosper your work done in his name, now and always. Amen.'

Casual vacancies

A casual vacancy can arise because an elected churchwarden fails to be admitted to office, or because one who has been admitted resigns, becomes ineligible to continue in office, or dies. Essentially the same procedure is used to fill the casual vacancy as the usual annual vacancy. The newly elected churchwarden must be admitted within three months. In practice, arrangements should be made for admission at the earliest possible opportunity; otherwise it is possible for a parish to be without a churchwarden for a considerable period of time.

The section concerning 'serious difficulties' noted above generates a further rule about casual vacancies (Section 4[8]): 'Any person chosen to fill a casual vacancy shall be chosen in the same manner as the churchwarden whose place he is to fill except that, where the churchwarden concerned was appointed by the Minister and the Minister has ceased to hold office, the new churchwarden to fill the casual vacancy shall be elected by a meeting of the parishioners.'

The fact that there are two of them

'The duties and rights of both Wardens are identical,' wrote the editor of the *Church Monthly* in the handy little *Hints for Churchwardens, Sidesmen and Others*, first published in 1908. He was right and it is still the case today. There is not a 'vicar's warden' and a 'people's warden' in the Church of England (though it is easy to see how these titles came about when the previously mentioned Canon 89 of 1603 was invoked). The duties and rights are identical, and no matter in connection with the office should be undertaken by either warden without consultation with his or her colleague, except in the cases of special emergency or the unavoidable absence of one or other warden. One of the first things you are going to want as a new churchwarden is the other churchwarden's contact details.

♦ 3 ♦

Responsibilities of office

What the churchwardens are responsible for

One of the ways to define the role of churchwarden is to say that he or she is there to assist the parishioners, the minister and the PCC to discharge the functions and duties laid on them by the Church of England and by the law of the land. These functions and duties divide into two: one area is clearly Christian in content and intent; the other, though largely directed towards Christian ends, is more like business administration or housekeeping.

The Canons of the Church of England contain a short section – two paragraphs of Canon E1 – dealing with the office of church-warden. They read as follows:

4 The churchwardens when admitted are officers of the Ordinary (i.e. the bishop). They shall discharge such duties as are by law and custom assigned to them; they shall be fore-most in representing the laity and in co-operating with the incumbent; they shall use their best endeavours by example and precept to encourage the parishioners in the practice of true religion and to promote unity and peace among them. They shall also maintain order and decency in the church and churchyard, especially during the time of divine service.

5 In the churchwardens is vested the property in the plate, orna-ments, and other movable goods of the church, and they shall keep an inventory thereof which they shall revise from time to time as occasion may require. On going out of office they shall duly deliver to their successors any goods of the church remaining in their hands together with the said inventory, which shall be checked by their successors.

What are these duties assigned to the office of churchwarden 'by law and custom'? If we start with law, we find churchwardens appearing in a number of Canons and Measures. The Care of Churches and Ecclesiastical Jurisdiction Measure 1991 (Section 4) lays upon the churchwardens the duty and responsibility of keeping proper records. It requires them to compile and maintain a full terrier (i.e. a list) of all lands appertaining to the church and a full inventory of all articles belonging to it. They are to do this in consultation with the minister. They are also to 'insert in a log-book maintained for the purpose a full note of all alterations, additions and repairs to, and other events affecting, the church and the lands and articles appertaining thereto and of the location of any other documents relating to such alterations, additions, repairs and events which are not kept with the log-book'.

Fabric and faculties

The same Measure lays on the churchwardens overall responsibility for the fabric. The relevant section (5) is rather long and is printed below in Appendix 2; in brief, it requires the churchwardens, at least once in every calendar year, to inspect the fabric of the church and all movables for which they are responsible and to produce an annual fabric report.

Responsibility for the fabric of the church requires an understanding of and compliance with faculty jurisdiction. The word 'faculty', generally speaking, signifies a privilege or special dispensation granted to a person to do that which by law they cannot do lawfully. In English ecclesiastical law the term is mainly applied to the authorization of works in and alterations to the fabric and contents of churches, and to churchyards. It was during the nineteenth century that faculty jurisdiction developed to near enough its present form. This was partly because of controversies over the introduction of certain High Church ornaments. For many years the obligation to seek a faculty was regarded as unquestionably binding in law. Phillimore summarized the position thus: 'No alteration, either by way of addition or diminution in the fabric or utensils or ornaments of the church ought, according to strict law, to be made without the legal sanction of the ordinary. That legal sanction is expressed by

the issue of an instrument called a faculty, and in no other way'
(2:1419).

The law requiring faculties for alterations in churches applies,
with certain limitations, to the setting up of tablets and monu-
ments in churches and churchyards, the removal of human
remains and the making of vaults and brick graves.

The obligation was given more concrete form by the
Ecclesiastical Jurisdiction Measure 1963, the Faculty Jurisdiction
Measure 1964 and the rules that followed from this Measure, and
then by the Care of Churches and Ecclesiastical Jurisdiction
Measure 1991 and the Faculty Jurisdiction Rules 2000. The obligation is that a faculty must be secured before any work or alterations are carried out to a church or its furnishings, or in the
churchyard or curtilage, or before anything is introduced into or
removed from a church. A faculty is granted, or refused, by the
chancellor of the diocese, and it is to the chancellor that application is made.

Most diocesan chancellors issue a list – known as the *de
minimis* list – of works that may be carried out without a faculty.
Such a list is specific to a given diocese and may vary from time to
time. In general, such a list is likely to include

1   works of routine maintenance on the fabric (up to a certain
    value and after consultation with the archdeacon), on
    electrical fittings and equipment, and on furniture;
2   movables (cruets, vases, surplices, cassocks, vergers' robes,
    authorized service books, Bibles, hymnbooks, replacement
    altar linen, temporary banners, replacement of worn-out
    flags, temporary items of decoration, such as Christmas
    trees);
3   furniture and fixtures in church halls, kitchens and toilets,
    fire extinguishers, replacement of carpets and curtains
    originally introduced by faculty;
4   routine tuning of organs and pianos;
5   bells: certain repairs to bellropes, pulleys, bearings, stays, etc.;
6   inspection and routine maintenance of clocks;
7   purchase and maintenance of lawnmowers;
8   certain items of work that may be authorized by the
    archdeacon.

The current diocesan list should always be referred to and the archdeacon or diocesan registrar consulted if there is any doubt about whether a matter requires a faculty.

In granting a faculty the chancellor takes into consideration the advice of the Diocesan Advisory Committee (DAC). Most DACs welcome early consultation about significant alterations to ensure that there are no difficulties with the formal submission. When a proposal is put formally to the DAC it has to include

1 full details of the proposed work;
2 plans, designs and specifications;
3 an estimate of the cost;
4 the comments of the inspecting architect;
5 the name of the architect employed (if not the inspecting architect);
6 details of all contractors;
7 photographs of the church;
8 photographs of any items to be introduced into or removed from the church.

When a proposal concerns an organ, bells or a clock, the papers are referred to a diocesan adviser for evaluation.

The DAC, after due consideration, returns the plans and other documents to the applicants (usually marked with the DAC's stamp), and the committee's certificate relating to the proposals. The certificate sets out the works considered by the DAC and gives the committee's recommendation. It can recommend, not recommend, or raise no objection. The second part of the certificate comments on the effect the proposals will have on the historical or archaeological significance of the building and advises on consultation with English Heritage, the local planning authority, National Amenity Societies, the Council for the Care of Churches and other persons or bodies.

Equipped with the DAC certificate, the minister and churchwardens as petitioners can now proceed to a petition for the faculty. They can do this even if the DAC does not recommend the grant of a faculty. The chancellor receives the advice of the DAC but is not bound by it. The standard petition form runs to 18 pages (13 to be completed by the applicants) and is one of the more daunting documents that a churchwarden may face. It is, however, prefaced by two pages of helpful notes, and diocesan registrars and archdeacons are always willing to answer questions where the petitioners have difficulties. Before completing the petition the petitioners need to ensure that the PCC has passed a resolution relating to the works and proposals and a certified copy of the resolution must go with the petition. The public notice part of the petition must be displayed outside the church, where it can be read by members of the public, for a period of 28 days before the petition is sent to the diocesan registrar.

This is the information you will need for every petition:

1 The date of the church.
2 If it is listed, its grade.
3 Information about whether it is or adjoins an ancient monument or is in a conservation area or a national park.
4 The name of the inspecting architect or surveyor.
5 The name of the architect or surveyor engaged for the works.
6 A statement of the cost of the works.
7 Details of the way in which the cost will be met, including the terms of any grant or offer of a grant.
8 Confirmation that other consents (planning authority, scheduled monument consent) have been obtained.
9 Information about bats. (Do you have them? Will the proposals affect them? Have you taken advice from English Nature?)
10 Details of contractors.
11 Timing of the work.
12 Arrangements if the church is to be closed.
13 A PCC resolution.
14 A DAC certificate.

The other information you require will depend on the sort of building you are dealing with and the sort of work you are proposing to do. If you have never seen a faculty petition, then call the diocesan registrar and ask for one. It is worth reading it through well in advance of any possible application.

Faculties take time and you need to look carefully at the possible timetable. You may have a number of constraints. Certain types of external work are better done in warmer weather, and other types of work cannot be done in the church at certain times because of weddings, festivals, etc. Then you need to consider the timing of PCC meetings (to pass a resolution), the time the DAC takes to respond, the period needed for the faculty citation, the constraints imposed by fundraising and grants, and the lead-in time of contractors.

When your proposal is nearing completion

1 check DAC dates and the likely waiting period for a certificate;
2 make sure you have a PCC meeting to pass a resolution (if not already done) and allow more time if necessary;
3 add on the period for display of the public notice (28 days);
4 check with the diocesan registrar on the waiting period for a faculty after the petition is received;
5 add on the lead-in time from receiving the go-ahead.

You then have the earliest date on which works can begin!

If the DAC does not recommend the proposals or there are objections to them once the public notice is displayed, then the period can be considerably lengthened. Tenacity is needed when it comes to faculty applications, but do not be tempted to do the work without a faculty.

A number of the cases in ecclesiastical law reported in the journal of the Ecclesiastical Law Society have concerned work undertaken without a faculty. (A selection from recent issues of the journal (up to issue 39) are also posted on the Society's excellent website at <http://www.ecclawsoc.org.uk>, and more recent case reports can be viewed at Cambridge Journals Online: <http://journals.cambridge.org/action/displayJournal?jid=ELJ>). Chancellor Bursell in the Durham Consistory Court (re St Giles, Durham, October 1998) reminded the parties, seeking a confirmatory faculty for various unauthorized works to a Grade I listed building (construction of a path and access ramp, the sanding of a wooden floor, alterations to pews, and the painting of the pulpit, altar rails, roof beams and corbels) of the provisions of Canon F13 and stated that 'because the Church of England and therefore its officers such as the minister and churchwardens are trustees of the heritage of the parish, the diocese and the nation, ignorance of the law and even well-intentioned breaches of the law cannot and will not be tolerated'. The PCC was ordered to pay the court fees.

Chancellor Coningsby, in the York Consistory Court (re All Saints, North Street, September 1999), was also concerned with works undertaken in a Grade I listed church, during restoration after a fire. Some work was undertaken that was not covered by the original faculty, including removal of a piece of a medieval pillar, and the petitioners sought a confirmatory faculty. The chancellor was 'critical of the churchwardens, PCC and parish architect for proceeding without authority of a faculty' and when he granted the faculty he ordered all the court and registry costs to be borne by the petitioners. Chancellor Coningsby was acting with the same intent as the Chancellor of Chichester, Judge Quentin Edwards QC, in the Chichester Consistory Court (re St Thomas à Becket, Framfield, September 1987) ([1989] 1 WLR 689, [1989] 1 All ER 170). In his judgment, he said:

> The churchwardens, and their successors in that office, are not, as lay men and women, liable to such proceedings [under the Ecclesiastical Jurisdiction Measure 1963]. They, however, should appreciate the pecuniary risks which they will run should they ever again execute such works without authority. A parochial church council is a body corporate (see s. 3 of the Parochial Church Councils (Powers) Measure 1956), and therefore no individual member of a council is personally liable for any debt or other liability of the body corporate which has been lawfully incurred. If, however, works to a church are executed without due authority, and so unlawfully, by the direction of a churchwarden or other member of the council that protection is lost. If, therefore a churchwarden, acting alone or with others, directs works to a church without the authority of an archdeacon's certificate or faculty he may expose himself to grave financial liability and loss. He may be ordered, personally, to pay the costs incurred in obtaining a confirmatory faculty. The archdeacon may himself seek a faculty authorising the undoing or alteration of the works and if such faculty be granted to the archdeacon the churchwarden may be ordered to pay all the archdeacon's

costs and expenses, viz. both his legal costs and the costs of the remedial works.

The importance of churchwardens and PCCs taking the time to understand the papers put before them – and not assuming that the lowest-priced option is always the best – is illustrated in the case re All Hallows, Harthill, heard at the Sheffield Consistory Court in January 2001. A Victorian stained-glass window in this Grade 1 listed building had been damaged by burglars. A modern window of modern design, similar to another modern window in the church, had replaced the damaged Victorian window, but no attempt had been made to comply with faculty jurisdiction and (presumably the lack of a faculty having been brought to the PCC's attention) a confirmatory faculty was now being sought. During the course of the hearing it became clear that a misunderstanding had taken place between the parish architect and the lay vice-chairman of the PCC. The architect had obtained quotations both to repair the window and to replace it. The PCC had accepted the lower quotation without realizing that this was the quotation to replace rather than repair the window. In relation to the faculty itself, the parishioners were split: the DAC positively recommended it, English Heritage opposed it, and the Council for the Care of Churches advised the chancellor to grant the faculty. Chancellor McClean ruled that there had been a genuine misunderstanding, and that the new window now formed part of a considered plan for the use of the north aisle. The confirmatory faculty was granted, but half the costs had to be borne by the parish architect who accepted that had there been no misunderstanding there would have been no need for a hearing.

Two cases, where churchwardens acted properly, illustrate the process required prior to the disposal of church property (re St Andrew, Trent, Salisbury Consistory Court before Chancellor Wiggs, January 2000 and re St John the Baptist, Halifax, Wakefield Consistory Court, December 2000). In both cases the churchwardens asked for a faculty to dispose of historic items in order to fund restoration works. The principles laid down were as follows:

1   The churchwardens have legal title to movable church property.

2 Church property cannot be sold without the consent of the PCC and the authority of a faculty.

3 Some good and sufficient ground must be proved to obtain a faculty.

4 A number of grounds might amount to 'good' grounds: the items to be disposed of might be too valuable to be kept in the church or they might be surplus to requirements and redundant.

5 The 'good' ground must also be 'sufficient' – that is to say, of sufficient weight to persuade the chancellor that a faculty should be issued; financial emergency relating to the fabric of the building could be a good and sufficient ground.

6 The chancellor must exercise his or her discretion in considering the evidence presented.

In the former case, Chancellor Wiggs allowed the sale of a pair of settles but required that the proceeds of the sale be placed in trust on terms approved by the chancellor in order to ensure that the income and, if necessary, the capital be applied to restoration work.

It is essential that churchwardens understand the part they play with regard to the care of churches and the faculty jurisdiction and, if they are to avoid legal penalties, follow the rules exactly.

Visitations and presentments

One part of the example of the churchwarden's declaration made before the bishop or his substitute (given on p. 36 above) may not be immediately comprehensible, namely: 'and will present such persons and things as are presentable by the Laws Ecclesiastical of this Realm'. The meaning of 'present' and 'presentable' in this context is to be found in Canons G5 (of Visitations) and G6 (of Presentments). The archdeacon makes an annual visitation – which does not usually mean that he actually visits the church, the incumbent and the churchwardens, but rather that the incumbent and churchwardens are cited to appear before him. In most dioceses, the archdeacon's annual visitation is also the occasion on which he admits churchwardens to office. It is the duty of the archdeacon to assist the bishop in his pastoral care and office, and in particular to ensure that 'all such as hold any ecclesiastical office ... perform their duties with diligence'. He therefore has to bring to the bishop's attention anything that calls for correction or merits praise. Canon G5 says that the archdeacon has the right to visit the archdeaconry committed to his charge 'at times and places limited by law and custom' and Canon C22 says that he is to do it every year, unless 'inhibited by a superior Ordinary' – that is to say, by someone (the bishop or, in rather rare circumstances, the archbishop) of higher authority. The preamble to the visitation required by Canon G6 is the Articles of Enquiry, historical examples of which we have already encountered. The Articles are delivered to the 'minister and churchwardens of every parish, or to some of them' and they provide the basis for the 'presentments' to be made by the minister and churchwardens. In simple terms, the archdeacon sends each parish a set of questions in order to gather information that might be useful to him. The minister and churchwardens have to use the questions as the basis for their answers and have to certify to the archdeacon that they have carefully considered their declarations, answers and responses and framed them 'advisedly and truly according to their consciences'. In addition, the churchwardens, being officers of the bishop, must 'present' to him, or to the archdeacon, either at the time of visitation or some other time, any matter which they believe should, according to the ecclesiastical laws, be brought to his attention. (In other words, the churchwardens' time-honoured duty of informing on the incumbent still, officially, stands.)

The kinds of question likely to be in contemporary Articles may include questions about the number and frequency of PCC meetings, whether your treasurer has attended deanery finance meetings, and whether your parish is supporting the diocese's overseas links. You are likely to be asked about the steps you are taking to safeguard children (in accordance with the Children Act) and to implement the Disability Discrimination Act. You may be asked about stewardship, pledged giving, Gift Aid and whether your parish complies with new accounting procedures. You might be asked about clergy expenses, the safety of clergy and their families – whether, for instance, there are smoke alarms in the vicarage. The questions are designed to ensure that you know about important matters affecting your parish and that your PCC is not ignoring matters that require attention.

Accompanying the visitation Articles of Enquiry may be what amounts to an annual returns pack, including material on parish finance and 'Statistics for Mission', all designed to provide the diocese with the information it requires.

First of all, the annual returns provide the basic information about the parish and its officers. Each year the diocese requires names and contact details for the churchwardens, the lay vice-chair of the PCC, the PCC treasurer and secretary, together with other financial officers (such as the chair of the finance and stewardship committee, if applicable, and the stewardship secretary or Gift Aid officer), the electoral-roll officer, the church's quinquennial inspector (also known as the inspecting architect) and the independent examiner or auditor. Every three years the return will also include the names of newly appointed deanery synod representatives.

The Return of Parish Finance and the Statistics for Mission are required by the Archbishops' Council. The financial information follows the pattern of the church accounts, examining income and expenditure for the previous financial year, January to December. The recently introduced statistical return asks for figures of baptisms, thanksgivings for birth of a child, marriages, blessings after civil marriages, funerals, Easter and Christmas communicants, normal Sunday attendance and number on the electoral roll. In addition, the return requires details of the number of adults, young people and children attending services (or Sunday school) in each week of October of the previous year.

Other responsibilities

Completion of the annual returns and answering the Articles of Enquiry are obviously tasks to be undertaken once a year. Other aspects of the churchwardens' responsibilities go on all year round; some of them are as old as the office itself. In 1908 *Hints for Churchwardens* included the following advice about lighting:

> The Lighting of the Church for Early Services and for Evening Services in the winter months will require supervision ... If there are many steps at the entrances, the outside lamps must be duly lighted at times of service, for in case of accident to any person

the Wardens might be sued for damages. The installation of Electric Light has been found to be a great convenience in Churches, both from an economical and sanitary point of view.

Today we might talk of risk management and compliance with disability legislation, but it amounts to much the same thing. On Sundays, while the minister has enough to do with officiating at services and preaching, possibly at a number of churches, it is the churchwardens together with the sidesmen who should take responsibility for the safety, warmth and well-being of the congregation. 'Nothing', says the writer of *Hints for Churchwardens*, 'adds more to the comfort of the congregation in cold weather than a properly regulated system of Heating the Church.' He also recommends the provision of 'a water-bottle and glass, and a bottle of smelling salts'. The churchwardens should consider carefully all aspects of the building for which they are responsible and the people who use it. They should look at the advice given by the Ecclesiastical Insurance Group and other church-focused insurance companies, together with the police and fire service. Here are some of the areas that should concern them:

1   Fire prevention, especially where there are votive candle-stands or where charcoal is used for incense.
2   Provision of fire extinguishers and training in their use.
3   The presence of trained first-aiders (St John Ambulance and the Red Cross both offer basic training courses).
4   Ready availability of a first-aid kit.
5   Provision of drinking water.
6   Availability of toilet facilities, especially in country churches.
7   Prevention of accidents: care must be taken over the use of candles, especially at Christingle, Candlemas, etc.; altar rails must be secure; carpets can create a tripping hazard, and so on.
8   Provision of a telephone in case assistance should be required.

The churchwardens are responsible for maintaining the good behaviour of persons in church. Canon E1 says: 'They shall also maintain order and decency in the church and churchyard, especially during the time of divine service.' It is usually sufficient to ask a man wearing a hat, for example, to remove it, it having been left on by accident rather than design. (A reference in the *Oxford English Dictionary* to *Blackstone* (Comm. I. xi. 395) of 1765 reads: 'A church-warden may justify the pulling off a man's hat, and without being guilty of either an assault or trespass.') Unfortunately there have always been, and are today, people intent on interrupting church services by unseemly conduct or by calling out. If this becomes a frequent occurrence, the churchwardens will need to seek police guidance. The wardens may request that a person leave the church building but they cannot compel by using any kind of force ('pulling off a man's hat' not being a recommended course of action for the twenty-first century). They are, however, entitled to bring the person before the magistrates.

'Order and decency' extend to those taking part in the service, both clergy and laity. Should some planned event or spontaneous action in worship give rise to offence, the churchwardens – who ought to have been consulted beforehand, if at all possible – will need to consider carefully what should be done. The normal course would be for them to speak to the incumbent and others concerned afterwards and, if necessary, make complaint to the archdeacon or bishop. They are, however, entitled to intervene during a service, but should do so only if absolutely certain that their intervention will be less offensive than what they are seeking to stop. (See Lord Stowell's strictures quoted earlier, on pp. 7–8.)

There is a general duty under canon law to ensure that all divine worship is reverent and seemly. The meaning of 'good order' is discussed at length by Chancellor Rupert Bursell in his book *Liturgy, Order and the Law*. He specifically deals with the responsibilities of churchwardens and summarizes them in this way:

[T]here is a common law right that permits anyone, whether a churchwarden or not, to remove a person who is disturbing divine service. A churchwarden, particularly, has a right to use reasonable force to remove anyone causing such a disturbance.

The churchwardens have a duty to maintain order and decency both in the church and churchyard, especially at the time of divine service; this may be fulfilled through the sidesmen, who are their assistants. If the minister is causing a disturbance, however, they intervene at their peril and should therefore only do so in the clearest of cases.[8]

Bursell wisely points out that standards of acceptable behaviour change over time, and the Canons do not state what is or is not permitted. He points to the vexed question of the wearing of a hat in church and holds that it is likely to be illegal today to remove a man's hat (as it might be being worn out of respect, as by a Jew, or for medical reasons) unless it causes offence other than by the fact of its being worn. The proper test of whether some action or behaviour requires intervention is whether it causes distress or disturbance to others. So, the wearing of a hat by a man during a service might cause more laughter than distress, but it might well be very distressing to others if worn during the singing of the Passion or at the consecration during a celebration of Holy Communion.

It is not only speech and action that can violate the principles of order and decency. The house of God should be clean and well appointed. It is inappropriate to have dirty altar linen, soiled vestments, dead flowers and filth in church. The ever reliable *Hints for Churchwardens* says this: 'SURPLICES ... dirty, ill-fitting, frayed, ragged or worn-out surplices are a great eye-sore, and with regard to anything and everything used in God's House it is good to remember the Apostolic injunction, "Let all things be done decently and in order".' The churchwardens therefore need to ensure that cleaning, both of the church itself and of the things used in it, is carried out regularly and efficiently.

The churchwardens are responsible for taking any offerings or collections in church. They may be assisted in this, as in other duties with regard to church services, by the sidesmen. They have responsibility for ensuring that the sums received are recorded in the register of services and will need to be aware that regulations in many dioceses – and good practice – require that the money be counted by no fewer than two persons, both of whom should sign the book. The churchwardens' immediate responsibility ends when the money has been paid to the treasurer or into the PCC's bank account.

The sidesmen (which term includes both men and women) are the churchwardens' assistants at church services; responsibility is delegated to them by the churchwardens for seating the congregation and maintaining good order and appropriate behaviour. The churchwardens should arrange the sidesmen's rota and ensure that they understand and carry out their duties. In a very busy church it can be helpful if the churchwardens have a deputy – at St Bartholomew the Great this person is known as the 'senior sidesman' – who takes responsibility for the rota and for the training of sidesmen. What do sidesmen need to know? Our training covers

1 the books and papers needed for services;
2 frequently asked questions about the church;
3 the collection and counting of money;
4 accounting for the money and putting it in the safe;
5 Gift Aid and stewardship envelopes;
6 location and use of fire extinguishers;
7 emergency evacuation procedure;
8 location of first-aid kit and identification of trained first-aiders;
9 how to deal with difficult people, including those who disrupt services or are disrespectful;
10 how to contact the police.

All sidesmen spend some time as trainees before taking full responsibility themselves.

The Parochial Church Council and its responsibilities

The powers of the PCC are set out in the Parochial Church Councils (Powers) Measure 1956, the composition and method of election in the Church Representation Rules 2006, and the 'General Provisions Relating to Parochial Church Councils' in Appendix II to those Rules. The PCC consists of

1 all clerks in holy orders beneficed in or licensed to the parish;
2 any deaconess or lay worker licensed to the parish;
3 in a team ministry, all members of the team;
4 the churchwardens;
5 such licensed readers on the electoral roll as the annual meeting shall determine;
6 all persons on the electoral roll who are members of the deanery or diocesan synods or the General Synod;
7 the elected representatives of the laity;
8 co-opted members, not exceeding one fifth of the representa-

tives of the laity or two persons, whichever shall be greater, who may be lay or ordained.

The situation is more complicated in parishes where there is more than one place of worship. Although the above is a lengthy list of categories of membership, the most important and the largest group will be the representatives of the laity. They should always form a sizeable majority.

Many PCCs now elect members for three years. If a PCC member becomes a churchwarden during a three-year term, the fact that he or she is now an *ex officio* member does not mean that the place to which he or she was elected becomes vacant (Church Representation Rules 47). A churchwarden, even if re-elected, could also have stood and been elected to the PCC. Equally, if a casual vacancy arises on the PCC during the term of office of a churchwarden, the churchwarden is eligible to stand for election. These points are particularly worth noting because a churchwarden who completes six successive terms in office can stand for re-election as churchwarden only under certain specific circumstances, but is not barred from rejoining the PCC as an elected member.

There have to be at least four meetings of the PCC a year, but in a busy parish there are likely to be more. The busiest of parishes will, however, rarely require more than six, unless it is engaged in some major project, and it is always worth remembering that a PCC meeting requires a great deal of preparation. Fewer, well-prepared meetings are better than more that are badly prepared.

Under the Synodical Government Measure 1969, which incorporates the provisions of the Parochial Church Councils (Powers) Measure, it is the duty of the incumbent and the PCC to consult together on matters of general concern and importance to the parish. The functions of the council include 'co-operation with the incumbent in promoting in the parish the whole mission of the Church, pastoral, evangelistic, social and ecumenical'. The PCC may also discuss matters concerning the Church of England or of religious or public interest, though it may not declare the doctrine of the Church on any question.

The minister is chairman of the PCC. In addition to members of the council, members of lay staff (an administrator, for example) or the PCC's professional advisers may attend PCC meetings with the consent or at the invitation of the council. The PCC is responsible for the care, maintenance, preservation and insurance of the fabric of the church, its goods and ornaments. The PCC has power to frame a budget and to take steps to raise and allocate moneys; it also has the power, jointly with the incumbent, to 'determine the objects to which all moneys to be given or collected in church shall be allocated'.

Meetings of the PCC are convened by the chairman. If one third of the membership signs a requisition asking him to call a meeting, he must do so within seven days (or, if he fails to do so, they can convene a meeting themselves). In the case of ordinary scheduled meetings, a convening notice must be displayed at least ten days beforehand, and a notice with an agenda should be sent to members seven days before the meeting is to take place. It is possible to postpone a convened meeting 'for some good and sufficient reason'. The quorum is one third of members. No business that does not appear on the agenda shall be transacted except by the consent of two thirds of the members present. Emergency meetings are governed by special rules. A majority vote decides business, and in an equal division of votes the chairman has the second or casting vote.

The council has to have a lay vice-chairman (who can be one of the churchwardens), a secretary, a treasurer and an electoral-roll officer. There must be a standing committee of no fewer than five persons. The minister and churchwardens are *ex officio* members of the standing committee, which 'shall have power to transact the business of the council between meetings thereof subject to any directions given by the council'.

The office of treasurer

The 'General Provisions Relating to Parochial Church Councils' appended to the Church Representation Rules 2006 contain just two specific references to churchwardens. The first concerns the office of treasurer. The PCC may appoint one or more of its members to act as treasurer solely or jointly, but in the event that the PCC is unable to do so (because none of its members is willing or competent to take on the role) the office shall be discharged by 'such of the churchwardens as are members of the council'. Second, with reference to the standing committee, the 'General Provisions' state that 'such of the churchwardens as are members of the council shall be ex-officio members of the standing committee'. (Prior to the Churchwardens Measure 2001 it was possible to be a churchwarden without being an actual communicant; as only actual communicants could be on the PCC, one or even both churchwardens might be ineligible to be PCC members. This is now changed, and both churchwardens will be members of the standing committee and responsible for acting as treasurer if no other member of the PCC is appointed to that office.)

Financial responsibilities

Whether or not either churchwarden (or both) also acts as treasurer, since they are members of the PCC as well as of the standing committee and, perhaps, of the finance committee, they have a wider responsibility for finance than merely overseeing the taking of collections, as described above. In particular, they should try to ensure that the PCC meets its financial obligations, including that of paying its specified contributions to the diocesan Common Fund ('the quota', which among other things meets the cost of clergy stipends and housing) and the payment of full clergy working expenses. It is to be expected that the churchwardens will report to the PCC on any meetings they have had with diocesan officers and make clear to the PCC what their financial obligations are.

The PCC has specific responsibility for accounting and financial reporting (more details about this are to be found in Chapter 5, 'New tasks for the twenty-first century'). In every parish legal provisions with regard to the PCC should be followed. In its areas of responsibility, the PCC should make decisions, implement them, and take responsibility for them – but the precise way in which business is carried out will differ from parish to parish.

Specific responsibilities of the minister

The minister is responsible for the performance of divine service. Other than a decision to change the authorized form of worship (e.g. from the Book of Common Prayer to *Common Worship*) the PCC has no responsibility for services. The priest or other minister should use a form of service authorized by the Church of England where one exists. The decision as to which type of service – i.e. BCP or *Common Worship* – is made by the minister with the PCC. It is for the minister to choose which of the permitted options may be used. The minister may also 'make and use variations which are not of substantial importance' in any authorized service and, in the absence of other authorized provision, use other forms of service. If there is any question about the appropriateness of such variations or whether they are consonant with the essential doctrines of the Church of England, the matter may be referred to the bishop for pastoral guidance.

In the choice of music the minister is required by canon to 'pay due heed to' the advice and assistance of the director of music, organist or choirmaster, but the final responsibility and decision in such matters as choosing chants, hymns, anthems and other settings rest with the minister. It is not the responsibility of the churchwardens or the PCC. The bells also fall under the authority of the incumbent: 'No bell ... shall be rung contrary to the direction of the minister.'

As the priest 'having the cure of souls', the minister is required to celebrate the Eucharist and to 'diligently administer the sacraments and other rites of the Church', to preach at least once each Sunday, to instruct parishioners in the Christian faith, to prepare candidates for confirmation, to visit the sick and to 'provide opportunities by which any ... parishioners may resort unto him for spiritual counsel and advice'.

An incumbent is supposed to reside in the parish; if living elsewhere, he or she must have a licence for non-residence, issued by the bishop.

The minister has overall responsibility for the life of the church and has no obligation to implement a PCC decision that he or she considers to be contrary to the best interests of the church, but the requirement for the PCC and incumbent to consult together should provide the safeguard that significant decisions are reached and implemented in an appropriate way, given the common trusteeship of property and money.

Checklists

Duties of churchwardens

1 To keep proper records, including terrier of lands and inventory of articles belonging to the church.
2 To keep a log-book of alterations, additions and repairs.
3 To inspect the fabric and produce an annual fabric report.
4 To deliver the fabric report first to the PCC and then to the Annual Parochial Church Meeting (APCM), including an account of the inspection they have undertaken and of all actions taken or proposed for the protection and maintenance of the building and the implementation of the quinquennial inspection.
5 To provide answers to the Articles of Enquiry, and complete the annual returns required by the diocese.
6 To present any matters they think ought to be brought to the bishop's attention.
7 To recruit, train and manage the sidesmen.
8 In conjunction with the sidesmen, to care for the safety, warmth and well-being of the congregation.
9 In conjunction with the sidesmen, to maintain order and decency in the church and churchyard.
10 To be responsible for the cleanliness and overall appearance of the church and everything used, or worn, in it.
11 In conjunction with the sidesmen, to take, count, and lock away or hand over to the treasurer collections in church.
12 To attend meetings of the PCC and of the PCC standing committee as *ex officio* members.
13 To act as treasurer if the PCC fails to appoint another of its members to this office.
14 To ensure that the PCC meets its financial obligations.
15 To collaborate and co-operate with the incumbent in the carrying out of all the above duties, and in enabling the incumbent to carry out his or her own specific duties.
16 To have a duty of care towards the incumbent.

Duties of the PCC

1 To care for, maintain, preserve and take out adequate insurance cover for the fabric, goods and ornaments of the church.
2 To agree a budget and to be responsible for the income and expenditure of the parish.
3 To maintain proper financial records and accounting procedures.
4 To prepare annual financial statements and an annual report, and present them to the APCM.
5 To arrange for independent examination or audit of the financial statements.
6 To consult with the incumbent on matters of general concern and importance to the parish.
7 To co-operate with the incumbent in promoting the mission of the Church.

Duties of the minister

1 To celebrate the Eucharist (or cause it to be celebrated in his or her absence) and administer the other rites and sacraments of the Church.
2 To be responsible for liturgy.
3 To have ultimate responsibility for music performed during the liturgy, in co-operation with the director of music, organist or choirmaster.
4 To preach (or cause to be preached) at least one sermon every Sunday.
5 To instruct parishioners in the Christian faith.
6 To prepare candidates for confirmation.
7 To visit the sick.
8 To be prepared to make himself or herself available to parishioners seeking spiritual counsel and advice.
9 To be diligent in prayer and study.
10 To chair the PCC, the PCC standing committee and the APCM.
11 To consult with the PCC.
12 To co-operate with the churchwardens.

♦ 4 ♦

Working with the minister

General good working practice

There is some overlap in certain of the responsibilities of the churchwardens and of the minister. The incumbent, for instance, is the person in whom the freehold of the church is vested, but possession is vested in the incumbent and churchwardens jointly. The incumbent has custody of the key, but the churchwardens have the right of access to the church for the proper discharge of their duties. Conversely, all the movable furniture and ornaments of the church are in the legal ownership of the churchwardens, but the clergy must be allowed the use of those objects necessary for their ministrations. It is for the minister to decide if the church can be used for plays, concerts and exhibitions, but he must obey any general directions from the bishop and, in case of doubt, must refer the matter to the bishop 'and obey his directions therein'. He or she must also take account of the views of the churchwardens who 'shall not suffer the church ... to be profaned by any meeting therein for temporal objects inconsistent with the sanctity of the place'.

No two priests are identical in their approach to ministry or their ways of working. Just as people in other walks of life, they enter on their vocation at different ages, they come with varied qualifications, and they are at various stages in their careers. A churchwarden has to work very closely with the incumbent or priest-in-charge of a parish and, if there is a very obvious differ-ence of approach likely to cause friction, it would be better not to serve as churchwarden in that case. It should generally be assumed that the clergy are committed, competent and professional in their ministry, and that they are aware of the stresses and strains, and possible pitfalls, that can beset them. Nevertheless, the clergy are also human beings and they welcome support, encouragement, praise and reasonable gratitude. The best people to offer this on behalf of the parish and congregation are likely to be the church-wardens and, in order to do so, they need to know something about how their priest works. They should also find out the answers to some basic questions, such as:

1 Is the priest getting sufficient time off?
2 Is he or she taking an adequate holiday from work?
3 Is he or she claiming for and receiving full working expenses?
4 Are parish expectations of the priest's role reasonable?
5 Is the priest finding time for prayer and for study?
6 Is he or she taking advantage of opportunities for in-service training and continuing ministerial education?

In addition to finding out what they can from the incumbent, the churchwardens may also ask diocesan officers for information about expenses, holiday entitlement, provision for retreats and study, and opportunities for in-service training.

The sort of support that the clergy will need will vary according to their abilities and experience. Three areas in particular need careful consideration: the new incumbent, the new incumbent who is also an incumbent for the first time, and the priest nearing retirement.

Working with a new incumbent

When he or she begins, the new incumbent needs particular support from the churchwardens in office, who will probably have served under the previous incumbent and who may well have been the parish representatives involved with the bishop or patron in making the appointment. Any new vicar, rector or priest-in-charge will need to ask questions and be given honest answers. Whatever loyalty the churchwardens might feel towards a former incum-bent, they must develop a loyalty to their new one.

In some cases, your new incumbent will also be a first-time incumbent: every parish priest has to be an incumbent (or priest-in-charge) for the first time. The first-time incumbent may well bring a wealth of experience, some of it from secular employment, some of it from a curacy. All of this will be useful but, despite some movements towards leadership or ministry teams, ordained and lay, the primary stress in many – probably most – parishes is on the rector, vicar or priest-in-charge, and the first-time incumbent is just that – in charge and responsible for parish leadership for the first time. That he or she should be able to command the loyalty and support of the churchwardens is particularly important at this point in his or her ministry.

The churchwardens have a moral duty to give wise counsel, to advise of problems and, when new ideas are put to the PCC, to protect the incumbent from ambushes. They should also check that their new incumbent has the basic knowledge and skills to undertake various administrative and managerial tasks. It should not be assumed that a priest will necessarily have been trained to

- understand church accounts;
- fill in marriage registers;
- chair PCC meetings;
- complete a PSA form;

or will be familiar with

- the Church Representation Rules;
- the Canons of the Church of England;
- the law relating to marriage;
- the division of parochial fees.

The churchwardens should therefore make sure that they are reasonably familiar with all of the above and be on hand to help if necessary, and provide guidance in enabling the incumbent to find the appropriate sources of information (see Appendix 5: Resources for the churchwarden).

As Chairman of the PCC the minister needs to be able to understand the accounts (which are likely to be fairly straightforward) and should certainly be familiar with the guidance given by the Archbishops' Council on church accounts in *The Charities Act 1993 and the PCC* (third edition, 2006). The sensitive churchwarden and/or treasurer will run through the accounts with the new incumbent *before* he encounters them at a PCC or standing-committee meeting and generally ensure that surprises are not sprung on him or her in public. It would also be a good idea for the churchwardens to take the new incumbent through the annual report for the last two or three years, during his or her early days in the parish. Not everyone is naturally good at chairing meetings and getting through the agenda in a business-like manner. A first-time incumbent more than other clergy needs a really good PCC secretary and a helpful, but not pushy, vice-chairman.

The churchwardens should ensure that the incumbent has an up-to-date copy of the Church Representation Rules (obtainable from Church House Bookshop – see <http://www.chbookshop.co.uk>). Vital for the procedures to be followed at the Annual Parochial Church Meeting, the Rules also contain an essential appendix of 'General Provisions Relating to Parochial Church Councils'. This appendix provides all the information needed about running the PCC, but does not set down its powers. These can be found in the Parochial Church Councils (Powers) Measure (see the extract that forms Appendix 1).

The Master of the Faculties of the Archbishop of Canterbury has produced a useful guide to the law relating to marriage in church (*Anglican Marriage in England and Wales: A Guide to the Law for Clergy*, obtainable from The Faculty Office, 1 The Sanctuary, Westminster, London SW1P 3JT). Guidance from the House of Bishops on the Marriage Measure 2008 can be downloaded from the Church of England website (<http://www.cofe.anglican.org/> – navigate to 'Information', then to 'Marriage and Family Issues', then 'Marriage and Divorce' and, finally, 'The Marriage Measure and Marriage Law Review'. The Registrar General has issued advice about marriage registers and certificates (Registrar General for England and Wales, GRO, Smedley Hydro, Trafalgar Road, Birkdale, Southport PR8 2HH). Fees are set out in a table distributed every year and are also to be found at <http://www.cofe.anglican.org/lifeevents/fees/>. The proportion of fees that goes towards the incumbent's stipend can be assigned to the diocese or retained by the incumbent, who then accounts for it to the diocese and to HMRC. For clergy who are not good with money, forms and tax returns, it is better to have the fees assigned *and* have all the payments made through the PCC treasurer. The PSA form replaced the earlier and more complicated PUN form. It is the annual return made by the clergy of fees, assigned or unassigned, and other clerical income, e.g. for chaplaincies, of working expenses and of expenditure in respect of the official house. It is very confusing for the clergy and for PCC treasurers that the returns are for the year to 31 March whereas church accounts are to 31 December. It is, however, important that the figures entered on the PSA form match those for the equivalent period in the church accounts.

Working with an old or retiring incumbent

The clergy may retire at 65 years of age and must normally retire at 70 (though they can obtain episcopal permission to go on a little longer in certain circumstances). Clergy pensions and housing can be a major source of anxiety for those approaching retirement. The clergy are all very different and we cannot predict how anyone will respond to the last few years before retirement. There are many very energetic clergy in their sixties and seventies but some will, of course, find that they are not able to do as much as they used to and may also be afflicted by poor health. Churchwardens need to be particularly alert to the needs of their clergy in the years approaching retirement, not least because clergy may want to devote more time to people and less to administration towards the end of their parish ministry.

Churchwardens – and not only those with an elderly incumbent – should be aware, and make sure that their minister is aware, of St Luke's Hospital for the Clergy, which provides free treatment for Anglican clergy and their dependent families. Founded in 1892 and completely modernized in 1994, it is now one of London's most up-to-date acute hospitals. Specialist services offered include a menopause clinic, stress management and couple counselling. It is based in Fitzroy Square, London W1, and the telephone number is 020 7388 4954. More details can be found on the hospital's website at <http://www.stlukeshospital.org.uk/>.

It is important for the parish that the transition be a smooth one, and churchwardens also need to consider their own timings in this respect. When the minister retires other church officers often think of retiring too, but it is not helpful for a new incumbent to find that the churchwardens are as new to the job as he or she is, or for new churchwardens to face the prospect of a lengthy vacancy just when they are trying to learn the ropes. The end of a ministry, especially a long one, is a time for stability on the one hand, and for openness to the future on the other. The new incumbent needs responsible people in place, even if one or more says that they would like to go after another year. The other side of the coin is that some church officers will want to hang on in order to prevent change; this is also unhelpful. Change is inevitable, made so by the different personalities of the clergy – the important thing is that this should be the kind of change that builds up the church.

The churchwardens have often become friends of the retiring minister and want to continue to be so. Equally, the newly retired minister will not necessarily want to sever all links with his or her former parish, but it is important to give it, and himself or herself, some space. It is also important to ensure that in subsequent conversations news of the parish does not become complaint about the new minister or implied criticism of the retired one. This is not easy but with some good will it can be achieved. The clergy, generally speaking, like to be invited back to their former parishes. The invitation should come from their successors, but there is nothing wrong with the churchwardens suggesting, after a space of two or three years, that the former vicar be invited back for some special occasion.

Churchwardens and a vacancy

During a vacancy, sometimes termed an interregnum (that is, after one minister has left and before another has taken office), the churchwardens and the rural, or area, dean are in charge of the parish. Together with any other clergy or readers attached to the parish, they will need to provide for the pattern of worship and pastoral care to carry on as near normally as possible, to ensure that the PCC covers the costs of services, to take care of any vicarage or other property of the parish and to ensure that fees payable to the diocese (i.e. for weddings, funerals, etc.) are collected and accounted for in the usual way.

If the living is not suspended, a new incumbent will be chosen by the patron of the living, together with the bishop and two parish representatives appointed by the PCC. In some cases the bishop is himself the patron. If the living has been suspended, the patron is prevented from presenting and the bishop may proceed to appoint a priest-in-charge. This would normally be done in consultation with the patron and the parish. The bishop may have been waiting for an incumbent to move or retire before proceeding to pastoral reorganization, and it may take some time before a new arrangement is agreed between a number of parishes.

To assist in the appointments procedure, the PCC should prepare a parish profile, describing the nature and traditions of the parish and the characteristics desired in a minister. Ideally this should have been prepared, or at least drafted, well in advance of the previous minister's leaving, as these are the kinds of decisions best made when people are not feeling under a time-pressure or anxious about the future. Every minister will have to leave eventually (even if it is for the heavenly realms), so it can never be considered a waste of time to prepare a parish profile and person specification.

If presentation to the living is not suspended, the PCC also needs to appoint the two parish representatives, who should be lay people but need not be the churchwardens. If the PCC feels the ministerial position should be advertised, they should ask the patron to do so. The PCC can also suggest the name of an individual they would like the patron to appoint, but they cannot insist on their choice. The parish representatives can, however, veto a candidate put forward by the patron, as can the bishop, but they should be prepared to give their reasons for doing so. In practice, the patron, bishop and parish representatives will usually endeavour to come to a mutual agreement. If, however, they do not succeed in doing so within a period of nine months, the right to choose the new incumbent passes from the patron to the archbishop.

When the appointment has been made, the churchwardens will be involved, together with the churchwardens of other parishes in the benefice, in organizing the service for the licensing or the institution and induction of the new minister. They will want to ensure, among other things, that invitations are sent to all the appropriate people, and that the broader community is represented.

Once the new minister is in place, churchwardens will need to exercise tact, sensitivity and self-restraint in relinquishing certain of the duties they undertook during the interregnum and in assisting others, such as lay readers and parish administrators, to do the same.

This is a very concise summary of what is involved in dealing with a vacancy. There are two helpful articles in issues of the *Ecclesiastical Law Journal*. The first, in the January 2001 issue, by David Parrott, entitled 'The Patronage (Benefices) Measure 1986: An Analysis of its Working in Practice', explores a number of models for the process of appointment and gives a step-by-step guide – 39 steps in all! – to the implementation of the Measure. The second, in the January 2002 issue, by Jonathan Redvers Harris, is entitled 'Living in Suspense: Problems and Solutions with Suspension of the Right of Presentation'. It tells a sorry and incomplete story of the united benefice of Puddingdale and is essential reading for the churchwardens of any parish facing a suspension.

CHECKLISTS

Things a churchwarden should do in the course of a year

Date	*Responsibility*
Prior to APCM	Present valid nomination to minister
Not later than 30 April	Election
Not later than 31 July	Admission
After, or at the time of, admission	Attend visitation
After admission	Receive terrier and inventory from predecessors and check them
January–March	Inspect church fabric and articles

March (probably)	Present fabric report to PCC
March–April	Present fabric report to APCM
April–May	Complete archdeacon's Articles of Enquiry and annual returns for diocese. If not re-elected, hand over terrier and inventory to successor

Things churchwardens should know

1 The contents of the Churchwardens Measure 2001.
2 Where to find information about

- filling in marriage registers and the law relating to marriage;
- completing a PSA form;
- the Church Representation Rules;
- the Canons of the Church of England;
- the division of parochial fees.

3 How to interpret the church accounts.
4 The whereabouts of registers of services, baptisms, confirmations, marriages and burials.
5 Whether Gift Aid envelopes are available in the church.
6 What happens to the collection during and after the service.
7 Who the inspecting architect is.
8 Whom to contact in the event of an emergency with the fabric.
9 When and how to apply for a faculty.
10 Whether the minister resides in the parsonage house or has a licence for non-residence.
11 When the minister's day off is (i.e. when not to try to contact him/her).
12 How many bank accounts the PCC has.
13 Whether there are any non-PCC accounts administered by the churchwardens.
14 The names of the independent examiners or auditors.

Things churchwardens should ask

1 Is the incumbent taking sufficient time off?
2 Is he or she taking adequate holidays?
3 Is he or she claiming for and receiving full working expenses?
4 Are parish expectations of the priest's role reasonable?
5 Is the priest finding time for prayer and for study?
6 Is he or she taking advantage of opportunities for in-service training and continuing ministerial education?
7 Are the service registers kept up to date?
8 What happens to the completed registers?
9 Is the collection being counted by at least two people?
10 Are the amounts received being entered in the service register?
11 Are the amounts being divided between 'open' and 'envelopes' (stewardship and Gift Aid)?
12 How does the money get to the bank?
13 Who has keys to the church?
14 Who has keys to the safe?
15 Where are the parish chequebooks kept?
16 Who are the account signatories?
17 Does the PCC meet at least four times a year?
18 Are the proper notices displayed?
19 Is an agenda sent out in good time?
20 Where are the signed copies of the PCC minutes kept?

♦ 5 ♦

New tasks for the twenty-first century

It is now generally expected of all institutions to exercise the virtues of transparency and openness, and the Church is no exception. This is, however, a new development in its history and calls for new approaches. In particular, various policies need to be enunciated, written down, agreed and made available for inspection – policies that in previous eras might merely have been 'understood', without the perceived need for formal agreement. Such developments result not only from the perception of transparency as a good thing; they have also come about as a means of protecting the officers and employees of institutions. As the General Synod working party on lay officers of the Church noted, we live in a litigious age. It is therefore important to be fore-warned and forearmed, to have such things as complaints procedures in place before the complaints arrive.

This section of the *Survival Guide* therefore considers various policy documents that churchwardens and PCCs should draw up. It also includes an introduction to fundraising, another constant and vital concern of contemporary parish life, as well as recommendations on how to compile the annual report.

As the people responsible for the mission of the Church of England in a parish or benefice, usually including the stewardship of a building or buildings and of money given to promote the work of the Church, the churchwardens and other PCC members carry significant responsibility. The Church is not funded by the State, though the building-repair grant scheme and English Heritage grants can involve considerable amounts of public money. Those who hold office in the church should be alert to the Seven Principles of Public Life set down by the Committee on Standards in Public Life (the Nolan Committee). These are:

1   *Selflessness*. Holders of public office should take decisions solely in terms of the public interest. They should not do so in order to gain financial or other material benefits for themselves, their family or their friends.
2   *Integrity*. Holders of public office should not place themselves under any financial or other obligation to outside individuals or organizations that might influence them in the performance of their official duties.
3   *Objectivity*. In carrying out public business, including making public appointments, awarding contracts, or recommending individuals for rewards and benefits, holders of public office should make choices on merit.
4   *Accountability*. Holders of public office are accountable for their decisions and actions to the public and must submit themselves to whatever scrutiny is appropriate to their office.
5   *Openness*. Holders of public office should be as open as possible about all the decisions and actions that they take. They should give reasons for their decisions and restrict information only when the wider public interest clearly demands.
6   *Honesty*. Holders of public office have a duty to declare any private interests relating to their public duties and to take steps to resolve any conflicts arising in a way that protects the public interest.
7   *Leadership*. Holders of public office should promote and support these principles by leadership and example.

The annual report

It has been the general policy of the Government to make PCCs accountable in the same way that registered charities are. Indeed, PCCs responsible for an annual income of over £100,000 will no longer be viewed as 'excepted' charities and will have to be registered with the Charity Commission. It is possible that when the Charities Act 2006 is revised in 2011, this threshold will be lowered and even more PCCs will have to register.

Even without registration, however, PCCs need to follow the regulations for charity accounting. The publication *The Charities Act 1993 and the PCC*, produced by a working party for the Joint Consultative Group of the Church of England and now in its third edition, provides guidance on how to fulfil the requirements of the

Charities Act and its associated Regulations and the Statement of Recommended Practice (SORP) for Charities. The book exists in two versions: *The Charities Act 1993 and the PCC: A Guide to the SORP Revisions* is aimed at PCCs with an annual income of £100,000 and over, while PCCs with an annual income of less than £100,000 are recommended to purchase *The Charities Act 1993 and the PCC: Preparing Receipts and Payments Accounts (SORP 2005)*.

The previous edition of this important document is still available for download, free of charge, from the Church of England's website at <http://www.cofe.anglican.org/info/papers/charact/charityact. pdf>, and it summarizes many of the requirements for PCCs:

The PCC is responsible for all parish finance, its management and control, including the appointment of a treasurer. While it may delegate some of its duties (for example, to DCCs), this does not remove its legal responsibilities. These include:

(a) Keeping 'proper accounting records', which are sufficient to show and explain all the PCC's transactions and must include a record of all relevant assets and liabilities. The records, together with the annual financial statements, must be preserved for at least six years from the end of the financial year to which they relate. The records must:
   (i) show and explain all the PCC's transactions;
   (ii) disclose the PCC's financial position at any time;
   (iii) enable the required accounts to be prepared;
   (iv) show on a day-to-day basis all receipts and payments and what they were for;
   (v) include a record of all assets and liabilities.
(b) Ensuring that the finances of the PCC are under its control and only delegated if the PCC can ensure that its wishes will be followed.
(c) Preparing an annual account (financial statements) and report, which shall be presented to the Annual Parochial Church Meeting in accordance with the requirements of the Church Representation Rules.
(d) Arranging for a suitable independent examination or audit of the financial statements.

One of the first steps in making PCCs accountable has involved the production, in addition to the annual accounts, of an annual report on the way in which the PCC has discharged its responsibilities (as specified in (c) above). Rather than looking on this as a chore, PCCs should see the new-style annual report and accounts as a tool. It can be used to publicize parish activities, to record achievements and to highlight needs. If the PCC applies for grants, it will usually need to submit a copy of the annual report with the application. Charities are also expected to report on their objectives, and the steps taken to achieve them, and to indicate how trustees are appointed and what training they are given.

The annual report will include two lists, the first of any staff, the inspecting architect, the PCC's bankers, and the financial inspector or auditor, and the second giving the membership of the PCC. If the members are elected for a three-year period it is helpful to indicate the date on which the term of office ends. See Example 5.1.

EXAMPLE 5.1 Lists in an annual report

Staff

Rector	The Reverend Henry Smith BD
Churchwardens	Donald Minchin
	Peter Herbert
Parish clerk	Edward Anderson
Verger	Tom Perch
Organist	Mary Swanson ARCO
Youth worker	Tony Carter
Inspecting architect	George Peters RIBA
Address	The Vicarage
	Any Parish
	Some County TW34 5GY
Bankers	HSBC
	Market Place
	Sometown TW24 7HY
Independent examiner	H. M. Neath FCA
	Anstee Nash
	62 Long Street
	Sometown TW23 9OK

Membership

Members of the PCC fall into three categories – *ex officio*, elected and co-opted. The rector and churchwardens, together with a reader and the representatives of the parish on the deanery synod, are *ex officio* members. Other members are elected for a three-year term at the Annual Parochial Church Meeting.

During the year the following served on the PCC:

Ex officio

The Reverend Henry Smith	Rector
Donald Minchin	Churchwarden
Peter Herbert	Churchwarden
Harry Poulter	Reader
Angela Reid	Deanery Synod (*2010*)
Michael Reid	Deanery Synod (*2010*)
Andrew Sweet	Deanery Synod (*2010*)

Elected	*Date of retirement/re-election*
Fleur Bell* (secretary)	*2010*
Monica Darbyshire*	*2009*
Michael Geddes	*2009*
Alexander Horsley*	*2010*
Nicholas Kempton*	*2011*
Charlotte Lincoln	*2010*
Janis Moss	*2010*
Anthony Lewis	*2011*
Monica Rayner	*2011*
Cheryl Shearman	*2011*
Nicholas Thomas* (treasurer)	*2009*
Richard Wake	*2009*

Co-opted

Simon Williams FRICS

*indicates members of the standing committee

The next section might provide details of the number and type of services held through the year. Example 5.2 comes from St Bartholomew the Great.

EXAMPLE 5.2 Details of services

There were 381 (2001: 388) services of all sorts during the year, of which some 130 were choral. There are normally three Sunday services: Sung Eucharist at 9.00 a.m., Solemn Eucharist at 11.00 a.m. and Evensong at 6.30 p.m. (with Benediction of the Blessed Sacrament once a month). On weekdays, there are celebrations of the Holy Communion on Tuesday at 12.30 p.m. and on Thursday (Fridays in Lent, and Red Letter Days) at 8.30 a.m. Various significant liturgical days are marked with appropriate ceremonies. Christmas is celebrated with numerous carol services and with Midnight Mass, Sung Eucharist and Solemn Eucharist. Holy Week begins with a Palm Procession from Charterhouse and includes full celebrations of the liturgy on Maundy Thursday, Good Friday, Holy Saturday and Easter Day. The average number of Sunday communicants has risen to an average of 76. Weekday communicants number approximately nine on Tuesday and 12 on Thursday.

Graphs can be useful to help people readily understand statistics. Sunday communicants can be displayed as in Figure 5.1, and the pattern over several years as in Figure 5.2.

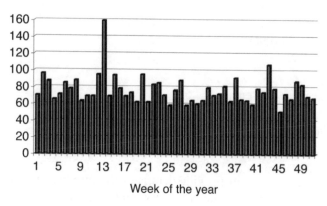

Figure 5.1　Sunday communicants

The electoral-roll numbers can be depicted in a similar way (see Figure 5.3), prefaced by a text something like this:

> The electoral roll was entirely renewed during 2007, having previously been renewed in 2002 (the usual six-year period having been changed to five years on this occasion, in accordance with a General Synod decision). Rolls have a tendency to rise during the six-year period, then to fall rather dramatically, before starting to rise again, as shown in the chart.

Congregations and others are rarely aware of the amount of work the clergy devote to the services, sometimes called occasional offices, that mark the passage of life: baptisms, weddings

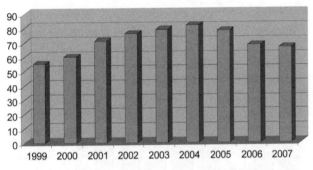

Figure 5.2   Sunday communicants 1999–2007

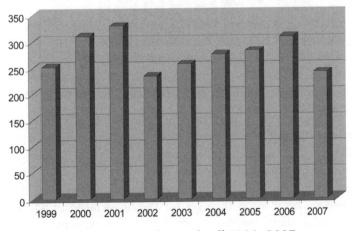

Figure 5.3   Electoral roll 1999–2007

and funerals. These too can be helpful expressed in chart form. A pie chart (Figure 5.4) is useful for this sort of information, and a further chart can map the pattern over a number of years (Figure 5.5).

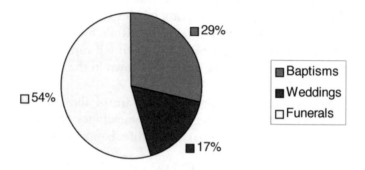

Figure 5.4   Occasional offices during the year

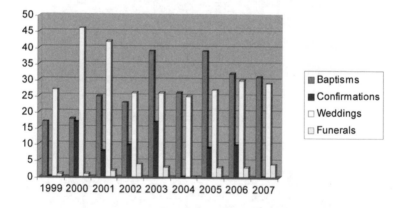

Figure 5.5   Occasional offices 1999–2007

The statistical section may then be followed by a review of the year, highlighting major events and particular achievements or challenges, and recording thanks to individuals and organizations. The annual report will also state how many times the PCC met during the year and list the main items of business that it discussed. The scene is then set for the financial information set out in accordance with the appropriate provisions governing annual reports and accounts.

Policy documents

The PCC is now responsible for a wide range of policies and will sensibly have agreed policy documents in place; among them should be the following:

- a statement of insurances;
- a policy to safeguard children and young people;
- a fire risk-management report and fire prevention policy;
- a disability access audit and policy.

It may also be helpful to have

- a procedure and policy for appointments (if staff are employed);
- a staff code of conduct;
- a disciplinary procedure;
- a complaints procedure.

Statement of insurances

The PCC is responsible for ensuring that there are adequate insurances, but members are often unaware of the policies, the valuation and the cost of insurances. The churchwardens should ensure that a report is made, in a format similar to Example 5.3, each year.

EXAMPLE 5.3 Report to the PCC on insurance arrangements

Purpose of the report
To advise members of the existing insurance arrangements for the church.

Insurance arrangements
The policy is within the City of London Deanery Group Scheme of Insurance with the Ecclesiastical Insurance Group.

Church insurance review
A review is carried out regularly by the Ecclesiastical

Insurance Group of churches within the City of London
Deanery Group Scheme. It last took place in September 2001.

Existing sums insured

Property damage section
Cover is provided for the perils of fire,
lightning, explosion, earthquake, storm,
flood, impact by road vehicle, aircraft,
escape of water, freezing of water, escape of
oil, falling trees, breakages of aerials, riot/civil
commotion, malicious damage, theft and
accidental damage. There are also various
extensions to this cover; for example,
equipment in the parish office, temporary
removal of items, equipment on loan,
minor building works, etc.
Buildings and contents combined sum insured   £12,862,500

Consequential loss section
Cover for loss of rent and/or additional
expenditure for the period in which repairs are
carried out to the premises following damage
covered in the Property Damage Section.
Limit of indemnity (any one event)   £25,000

Money section
Cover for loss of money while
(a) in course of transit or in a bank night safe   £2,500
(b) while being counted at premises or home of
    church officials   £2,500
(c) in a locked safe at the premises   £2,500
(d) any other loss   £250

Theft by church officials section
Cover for misappropriation of church funds
Limit of indemnity (any one claim)   £10,000

Liabilities section
The following covers are supplied as standard:

Employers' liability	Limit of indemnity	£10,000,000
Public liability	Limit of indemnity	£5,000,000
Products liability	Limit of indemnity	£5,000,000

Legal expenses section
Cover for legal costs incurred in defending a
criminal or civil action

Limit of indemnity   £100,000

Personal accident section
A range of benefits for employees/volunteers
who are injured while carrying out duties on
behalf of the PCC.

Other insurances
Engineering Insurance Policy issued by
Ecclesiastical in association with Haughton.
This policy covers the hot-water boiler at St
Bartholomew the Great. An annual inspection
is carried out each year by Haughton.

Loss or damage to boiler from sudden or
unforeseen causes:
Limit of indemnity (excess £100)   £500,000
Fragmentation cover:
Limit of indemnity (excess £100)   £100,000

Display of employers' liability insurance
The current certificate is displayed on the notice
board in the west porch.

Policy on child protection and young people

A PCC policy, though tailored to the needs of the local parish,
must be based on the recommendations of the *Church of
England House of Bishops Policy on Child Protection* and any

guidelines issued by the diocese (each diocese may have its own variations), as well as meeting the requirements stated under the Children Act 1989 and the Home Office's guidelines. The policy may refer to other publications and the provisions contained in them, and it should be reviewed annually. Staff and volunteers dealing with children will need to be properly recruited, trained and supported. They will also need to be familiarized with the Church's Policy on Child Protection, the Church of England House of Bishops Policy on Child Protection and the diocesan guidelines. The PCC must also ensure that it has adequate insurance cover, including public liability insurance, for all activities organized by the church and held at the church that involve children. (The Children Act 1989 defines a child as a person under 18 for most purposes; the category 'young people' seems to be used primarily by the Church and is generally taken to refer to people between the ages of about 15 and 18, while church registers include columns for those under 16.) A policy statement will look something like Example 5.4 (depending on diocesan guidelines).

EXAMPLE 5.4 Policy for the protection of children and young people

The PCC of this church agreed and adopted the following policy on Child Protection and Young People at its meeting held on 26 September 2003.

1 We commit ourselves to safeguard the welfare and protection of all young people who come to this church.
2 We recognize that our work with children and young people is the responsibility of the whole church community.
3 We accept and endorse the principles of the Children Act 1989 and the House of Bishops Policy Statement *Protecting All God's Children* (2004).
4 We undertake to exercise proper care in both the selection and appointment, and in the support, of those working with children.

5 We wish to support parents and those who have responsibility for bringing up children.

6 The PCC's Working Party for the Protection of Children and Young People has been appointed as our Children's Advocate as described in the Diocesan Child Protection Guidelines.

7 A copy of the Diocesan Child Protection Guidelines is held by the rector's secretary.

8 This policy will be reviewed annually.

Fire precautions and risk management

Free-standing churches without offices or staff working on the premises are not covered by any fire or safety legislation, but proper fire precautions and an evaluation of risk of fire are sensible steps and should be undertaken. Churches that are also workplaces are covered by legislation concerning health and safety at work and are subject to inspection by the local fire brigade.

These regulations impose health-and-safety requirements for fire-precautionary matters in the workplace. It is necessary for the PCC to undertake a fire-risk assessment and keep it available for inspection by the fire authority. This entails a structured and systematic examination of the workplace to

- identify hazards from fire;
- decide if a hazard is significant;
- decide who is at risk;
- decide whether the existing fire precautions are adequate;
- make an action plan to minimize the hazard.

A written emergency plan then has to be prepared to indicate the action that people should take in the event of a fire. This plan must be kept for inspection by the fire authority.

Together the fire-risk assessment and emergency plan should

- identify all the significant fire hazards;
- identify who is at risk from each fire hazard;

- evaluate existing control measures to see whether they reduce risk to a tolerable level;
- determine what additional measures are required;
- describe the means of escape from the premises in case of fire.
- describe the means of detection and of giving warning in case of fire;
- describe the means of fighting the fire;
- include planning for an emergency;
- provide for training, information and instruction to staff about fire precautions in the workplace;
- provide for effective maintenance and testing of fire-safety equipment and precautions.

An assessment will almost certainly identify some areas of concern. There may be a tension between the advice of crime-prevention officers (e.g. reducing the number of exits) and the fire regulations, and advice may be needed in establishing a balance between fire-exit procedures and security of the building against theft and vandalism. There is also a cost implication in the provision of acceptable means of escape (especially from the more difficult parts of a church, e.g. the bell tower, the organ loft), and the installation of smoke detectors and alarms. There must also be adequate means of escape when the church is full for services or special events, and sidesmen, ushers and others need training in the use of fire extinguishers and in marshalling a crowd. A PCC fire policy might be set out as in Example 5.5.

EXAMPLE 5.5 Fire policy

The Parochial Church Council is committed to:

1 The protection of life in the event of a fire.
2 Protecting the buildings and contents of the church against fire.
3 Developing a fire-safety strategy for the church based on a detailed fire-safety audit and risk assessment.
4 Ensuring compliance with all statutory controls in respect of fire safety, and establishing effective liaison

with the local fire service and the church's insurers.

5 Ensuring that measures provided for fire safety are compatible with the conservation interests of the building, as far as is practicable.

6 Making all staff and volunteers aware of the importance of fire safety and ensuring that they receive appropriate training so that they can discharge their responsibilities effectively.

7 Ensuring that the required standards of fire safety in the church are regularly audited and inspected.

8 Operating a management structure within which the fire-safety policy can be implemented and fire safety can be effectively managed.

9 Reducing the danger from fire as far as is practicable and reasonable.

10 Integrating fire-safety policy into general health-and-safety policy.

11 The fire-safety policy for the church is to be reviewed regularly and updated as necessary to reflect changes to the use, management or fabric of the building, or changes to the statutory controls that are applicable.

Fire-risk management involves looking carefully at areas that combine a source of ignition with combustible material, identifying risk and taking steps to reduce it. An inspection at one church gave rise to the risk report given in Example 5.6.

Disability access and audit

'If there was a wedding in your church where the bride was a wheelchair user, the groom's mother blind, and a number of guests had severe hearing loss or learning difficulties, would the facilities available meet their needs?' This was the question put to PCCs by a DAC in order to begin the exploration of disability access. It is not an optional extra. The Disability Discrimination Act 1995 states that is unlawful for a provider of services to discriminate against a disabled person in refusing to provide, or in deliberately failing to provide, the disabled person with any service that he or she provides, or is

EXAMPLE 5.6 Report on fire risk at St X's Church

Area	Risk	Action to be taken
Crypt	Low risk. We were concerned about the amount of paper rubbish in the crypt and elsewhere in the church.	Removal of rubbish.
Kitchen	The gas stove, the iron and the dryer provided possible sources of ignition. The stove is used for lighting charcoal for incense. We were concerned about the amount of flammable material, esp. newspapers, together with candles. The fire extinguishers were not easily accessible.	Removal of rubbish. Removal of candles. Regular cleaning of dryer filters. Iron to be unplugged when not in use and not to be left unattended. Relocate fire extinguishers. Replace black fire extinguisher with a red one.
Sacristy	Low risk.	Flammable materials not to be kept in sacristy.
Toilets	Low risk.	
Store	Medium risk. We were very concerned about the general disorder and disarray. Flammable materials and candles are kept here as well as paper towels and cardboard.	Candles should be moved out of the store room; we suggest that better use could be made of the cupboards in the corridor. The room should be tidied and reorganized.
Lady Chapel	Low risk. We were satisfied that the votive candlestand did not increase the risk. A falling candle would fall on to tiles and there was no fuel for fire. Candles should, however, be extinguished when the church is closed. The altar candles burn only when people are present in the church. The organ should be unplugged when not in use.	Extinguish votive candles before closing church. Unplug organ when not in use.
Verger's vestry	Medium risk. We were again concerned about the mix of materials: rubbish, paper, candles and tapers.	Tidy up. Remove candles.
Vestry	Low risk. Despite the storage of candles here and the use of tapers for lighting candles we are clear that there is little risk *if proper procedures are followed* by servers.	Removal of flammable materials from candle cupboard. Removal of combustible materials around safe (where tapers might be dropped).
High Altar	We thought that the votive candlestand increased the risk *very slightly* and that the kneeler should be moved along to leave a clear space and reduce the possibility of a lighted candle falling on it (rather than next to it) and setting fire to it.	Kneeler to be kept moved towards south pillar.
Switch room	Low risk. Although the electrical intake is here, there is very little combustible material.	Keep clear of combustible material.
Office	Low risk. There are a number of pieces of electrical apparatus in the office and an abundance of combustible material but all safety precautions are carried out and plugs, etc., are not overloaded.	

prepared to provide, to members of the public. The expression 'provision of services' includes the provision of any goods or facilities and access to and use of any place that members of the public are permitted to enter. Churches, therefore, fall under the provisions of the Act and it would be unlawful to discriminate, whether deliberately or by an act of omission, against any disabled person, whether in regard to worship or in access to a building. The Act goes further in stating:

> Where a provider of services has a practice, policy or procedure which makes it impossible or unreasonably difficult for disabled persons to make use of a service which he provides, or is prepared to provide, to other members of the public, it is his duty to take such steps as it is reasonable, in all the circumstances of the case, for him to have to take in order to change that practice, policy or procedure so that it no longer has that effect.
>
> Where a physical feature (for example, one arising from the design or construction of a building or the approach or access to premises) makes it impossible or unreasonably difficult for disabled persons to make use of such a service, it is the duty of the provider of that service to take such steps as it is reasonable, in all the circumstances of the case, for him to have to take in order to –
> (a) remove the feature;
> (b) alter it so that it no longer has that effect;
> (c) provide a reasonable means of avoiding the feature; or
> (d) provide a reasonable alternative method of making the service in question available to disabled persons.

A PCC has a duty to inspect the building or buildings used for its various purposes and to appraise accessibility, judging against predetermined standards (e.g. of space needed for wheelchair access). The PCC will certainly focus on the church building and the extent to which steps or other obstacles limit access, but must also be aware that a disabled person could be prevented from joining in activities (such as Bible study, PCC meetings, etc.) that took place in a private house that was not accessible for such a person.

Alteration to a building, especially an historic building, to remove the obstacle created by a physical feature creates all sorts of difficulties and adds a further burden of cost, but the PCC is required to carry out an access appraisal and to take all reasonable steps to provide access.

A PCC should

1 discuss disability access and appoint an 'access officer' to be responsible for ensuring that the matters raised are dealt with. The officer should talk to disabled people and their carers, and to members of the congregation and visitors who use wheelchairs and pushchairs, or have difficulty with hearing or with steps, etc.;
2 look for simple solutions: changing the way you do something is simpler than changing the building;
3 consult the inspecting architect or surveyor about possible structural alterations;
4 draw up an action plan, with a timetable and a budget;
5 consult the archdeacon;
6 seek the advice of the DAC and others, in the normal way, before proceeding to a faculty application.

Employment

PCCs are rarely used to being employers and might be advised to seek legal advice before employing anyone for the first time. Large firms of solicitors will often be willing to provide advice on this *pro bono*. What is essential is that, in appointing anyone to any job, voluntary or paid, the employer's expectations are clearly set down in an exchange of letters, that there is a probationary period and a means of appraisal, and that there is a means of terminating the arrangement amicably if circumstances change or standards are not met. The PCC is the employer of paid staff working for a church and carries the same legal responsibilities as any other employer. With advice, the PCC should agree

• the job description;
• the terms and conditions, including pay and pensions;
• the method of appointment (advertisement, short-listing, interviews, referees);
• the means of appraisal.

The PCC should then go on to draw up

- a disciplinary procedure;
- a grievance procedure (to be used by staff);
- a code of conduct to guide staff in carrying out duties.

Complaints policy and procedure

Jesus' command to his disciples is that they should love one another with his own love for them as the standard and example. This 'law of love' extends to the life of the church, but we know from the New Testament record that there could be disagreement, discord and dissension within the Christian community and that the Apostle Paul frequently had to deal with it. The important thing emerging from his letters is that the gospel is paramount and we must not allow anything to deflect the church from its apostolic mission. Disagreement should therefore be dealt with swiftly and effectively and in a way that is consistent with the requirement to be united in the love of Christ.

All churches receive complaints from time to time. These may be directed to the bishop, archdeacon or rural (or area) dean, or directly to the incumbent or the churchwardens. While not encouraging complaint, we should remain open to genuine dissatisfaction and all complaints should be treated seriously and investigated fully and fairly. Most complaints can be dealt with informally but a formal procedure can aid resolution. A good system is that of appointing someone who is generally respected, but is not a member of the PCC, to be a complaints officer. If that person has some legal training or related experience, so much the better. With these principles in mind (and probably including them in a preamble to a complaints policy), a PCC might adopt a policy like that in Example 5.7.

EXAMPLE 5.7 Policy on complaints

We will always try to deal with complaints addressed to the minister, churchwardens or other officers informally and in an amicable fashion where possible. Complaints addressed to the bishop, archdeacon or area dean are generally referred back to the minister but must be dealt with in whatever way the bishop directs.

Our complaints procedure is divided into informal and formal stages. We would expect that the majority of complaints can be dealt with informally.

Complaints will be dealt with on as confidential a basis as possible, but the person who first receives a complaint will need to discuss it with those who can resolve it, so anonymity and total confidentiality cannot be expected.

The procedures set out below are for complaints made by persons entered on the church electoral roll, members of the congregation, visitors and others who participate in the life of the church or receive its ministry. Other procedures will be set up to deal with specific types of complaint, e.g. by a member of staff.

A copy of this document will be given to any person who initiates a complaint.

Informal stage

If anyone (other than a paid employee of the church) wishes to make a complaint, it should normally be addressed to the minister. If it is a complaint concerning the minister, it should be addressed to the churchwardens. Many concerns arise from misunderstandings and can be resolved by simple clarification. If the minister or churchwardens consider a complaint too serious for the informal stage, then they will immediately commence the formal stage. If the complainant is not satisfied with the way in which a complaint is dealt with during the informal stage, then he or she may request that the formal stage be initiated. The churchwardens and other officers are required to bring all complaints to the attention of the minister.

Formal stage

The formal procedure begins with logging the complaint in a confidential log-book, which will contain the date of the complaint, a brief outline of it, a summary of the steps taken to resolve it and the outcome.

The complaint will then be passed to a 'complaints officer' (a designated person who is not a member of the PCC). The complaints officer or a person or persons nominated by him or her (who shall not be members of the PCC) will investigate the complaint. The complaints officer will, as necessary, seek the advice of the diocesan registrar.

A confidential file will be kept on each individual formal complaint while it is investigated.

The complaints officer will advise the complainant if a complaint that alleges breach of the ecclesiastical law should be addressed to another person or body.

The complaints officer will determine what steps should be undertaken to resolve the complaint.

Members of staff and officers of the church against whom a complaint is made will be kept fully informed of the investigation being made and will be given a written statement at the end of the investigation.

The person making the complaint will be informed in writing of the outcome of the investigation and the action taken.

Any complainant who is not satisfied with the way in which a complaint is dealt with is at liberty to renew the complaint to the diocesan bishop. The complaints officer shall then send to the bishop a copy of the confidential file and an account of his or her investigation of the complaint.

Introduction to fundraising

It is not to be assumed that churchwardens should be single-handedly responsible for carrying out the fundraising for their church, but they should be aware of the issues involved and closely concerned with the strategies for raising money.

There are two aspects to be considered: revenue funding (making sure there is sufficient income to maintain the life of the church and to deal with routine maintenance of the fabric) and fundraising for specific projects – usually, though not always, projects to do with major fabric works.

Revenue funding

This is the responsibility of the whole congregation, and especially of the churchwardens and PCC, whose job should include raising the congregation's level of awareness as to the necessary expenditure of the parish and the income required to maintain that expenditure. Means to produce that income will include

- pledged giving (stewardship);
- making full use of Gift Aid;
- taking open collections at services;
- having a donations box in church for visitors;
- the regular round of small fundraising events (bazaars, jumble sales, etc.) – if yours is a parish where such events are an enjoyable tradition.

Without going into detail on any of the above – most parishes will have various strategies already in place – it is worth pointing out that it is useful if the PCC appoints a stewardship secretary (who should not, for preference, also be the treasurer), whose job it will be to keep track of amounts raised through planned giving, and to manage the Gift Aid audit trail and deal with the Inland Revenue. You will also want to decide how often you want to organize a stewardship campaign – probably every few years, or whenever you become aware of a growing number of new members of your congregation who have not yet signed up for pledged giving or who do not know what 'stewardship' means in this context. (It is a rather unfortunate term, in that it does not and should not apply only to money, but also to the management and offering to God of our time and talents. Focusing too much on these latter aspects, however, can become an excuse for never confronting the issue of money and the church's need for financial support from its members.)

It is also worth mentioning that the donations box should not only be as secure as possible (and emptied at regular intervals) but should also carry a clear sign of the amount requested from every visitor. People respond to requests for specific amounts of money; they cannot know, without information, what it costs to run the church. You need to tell them what is expected, or they will understandably put in only small change. If you are in the fortunate position of being regularly visited by overseas tourists, it may also be worth your while stressing that you accept foreign currency, particularly euros and American dollars. It is usually possible to arrange conversion into sterling with your bank at no charge.

Fundraising for specific projects

When a major fundraising initiative is needed, the usual round of collections and small events will not be enough. One temptation can be to go for the appointment of a professional fundraiser, and in some cases this may be the right path to go down, but it is worth bearing in mind two things. First, the fees a professional fundraiser is likely to charge will significantly increase the amount of money you need to raise. Second, once the specific project has ended, you will lose the expertise of the professional fundraiser. There are some very good courses on fundraising offered by such bodies as the Charities Aid Foundation and the Directory of Social Change, and it is always worth considering whether there is some- body in your congregation or associated with your church in some other way who would be willing and able, with appropriate training, to become your part-time (paid or even voluntary) fundraiser. That way the church's initial outlay is considerably less, and you will not be in danger of losing the expertise acquired by the fundraiser, who will be appointed for not only one project.

Whether you decide to use a professional or to train one of your congregation or a member of your church staff to undertake this role, you should not leave this person in isolation or imagine that you can happily leave all the work to him or her – or even to a fundraising committee. One of the first things a fundraiser is likely to do is to come to you for information. He or she will need to find out from you complete details of the project you are under- taking – the timings and precisely when funding is needed – but will also want to ask about possible sources of income. Whom do you know who might be prepared to make a donation? What connections do you, or anybody else in the parish, have with the trustees of various charitable trusts? Whom have you approached for money in the past and who might be willing to give again? Who should not be approached? (Another argument against appointing a professional fundraiser is that you may think you could have thought of these questions yourself, rather than paying someone else to do it, and that the amount of work involved in answering them is the same, whether you are paying someone to ask them or not.)

A second temptation when undertaking a major fundraising campaign is to concentrate all the efforts and time of your committed church members on organizing an event of some sort, from a bazaar to a ball. Events have their place in fundraising, but they can also become a form of 'displacement activity'. The organization involved in putting on an event keeps people busy and makes them feel useful – irrespective of the amount of money they actually raise. Before launching into any kind of fundraising event, it is vital to cost it properly – and conservatively. If it is an event for which you intend to sell tickets, never estimate the profits on the basis of a 100 per cent take-up. Estimate 75 per cent, and you will be closer. Take into account the costs of publicity and the payments that need to be made to any professional caterers or entertainers. Above all, look at the manpower involved in putting on an event and question whether this is the best use of your resources. You may conclude that it is, in which case go ahead. But you might also consider whether you are involving yourselves, your PCC members and your congregation too much in 'church-centred' events. That may sound a rather odd thing to say, but it is important to remember that where fundraising is concerned (and, one might add, where the spread of the gospel is concerned) no contact is wasted. In your role as churchwarden, you have a part to play not only in your church but in your wider community. The people you meet in your professional work, in your leisure activities, in local politics, will be affected by knowing that you are a churchwarden and that this is a very important aspect of your life. And it is through getting to know a wide circle of people – outside the church as well as in it – that you will increase the pool of possible donors. This does not at all mean that you should be asking for money all the time – far from it; nothing can be more off-putting. It does mean that you increase the chances of meeting someone who has a way in to a source of funding, and who may be prepared to exercise that influence on your church's behalf.

You need to take care when collecting information about

donors and potential donors that you abide by the rules of the Data Protection Act. Anyone processing personal data must comply with the eight enforceable principles of good practice, which are that information must be

- fairly and lawfully processed;
- processed for limited purposes;
- adequate, relevant and not excessive;
- accurate;
- not kept longer than necessary;
- processed in accordance with the data subject's rights;
- secure;
- not transferred to countries without adequate protection.

When writing to people – such as members of an organization connected to your church – you should ensure that you tell them how you obtained their names and addresses, that you are using them only for the purposes of this mailing (i.e. you will not make them available to anyone else) and how you will subsequently use any information collected about them as a result of the mailing.

As a not-for-profit organization, you will not normally need to notify the Information Commissioner. Further information about Data Protection requirements can be found at <http://www.ico.gov.uk/> or by writing to the Information Commissioner, Wycliffe House, Water Lane, Wilmslow, Cheshire SK9 5AF. Further written guidance on the exemption for not-for-profit organizations is available by telephoning the notification helpline on 01625 545 740.

A major source of potential funds is the many charitable trusts that exist in the UK and can be researched through such bodies as the Directory of Social Change, the Charities Aid Foundation and the Charity Commission. It is implicit in what has been said above about contacts and networking that shooting off letters is not the only, or the best, way of approaching a potential grant-giving body. Sometimes – as in the tight scheduling involved in raising money for the 'implementation stage' of a project supported by English Heritage – there may be no time to do much more than write letters to the trusts you have identified, but ideally you should prime your target before sending off your begging letter.

Find out who the trustees of a particular body are, research their interests, what they do, where they live, what their hobbies are (you can glean a lot of information from reference works such as *Who's Who* or Debrett's *People of Today*) – and circulate these details to members of your PCC and committed congregation. When you find someone who knows a particular trustee, who belongs to the same club or professional organization, perhaps, or has children who go to the same school, see if you can make an indirect approach before sending off your official letter. It is similar to trying to get a book published – it helps enormously if you can guarantee that your letter of application will actually be read, and that it can be distinguished from the pile of similar letters, and it is personal contact that is likely to ensure that this will happen.

Approaching charitable trusts is of course only one possible avenue of fundraising, and you should not neglect your sources of income nearer home – your parishioners and members of the local community. Here it is important to try to capture the imagination. We are all bombarded with requests for money all of the time, from the major national appeals – Comic Relief, and so on – to the beggar on the doorstep or the charity worker who stands on the pavement and asks people as they hurry by on their lunch-hour: 'Can you spare a minute for the elderly? or the blind? or cancer sufferers? or dogs?' It is no wonder that people become inured to requests for financial assistance, however worthy the cause. So you need to find some way of appealing to people that both interests them and makes a positive response easy.

One of the PCC members at St Bartholomew the Great came up with the inspired idea of asking people to pay ten pence a year for each year of the church's life. As this particular appeal was launched in 2001 and the church was founded in 1123, this meant that the sum being requested from each individual was £87.80. This unusual and very specific sum somehow caught on. It was well under £100, and there was an option to pay in three instalments, so it did not feel too enormous, and it had its own kind of logic. People could relate to the idea of 'ten pence a year' and a high proportion of people responded. The appeal mailing also included a Freepost envelope for the replies – a very worthwhile investment, as is any stratagem that makes giving relatively easy. Every contribution that was eligible was also Gift Aided, of course, and it was also stressed that any contribution, no matter how small, would be gratefully received.

A particular role that churchwardens may play is that of thanking people for their contributions. A written note from the incumbent and/or churchwardens to express thanks for the support of every donor is not only a mark of courtesy, but may bear fruit in the future, as someone who has been personally thanked is more likely to respond to further appeals than are those who feel their donation has been taken for granted.

Another role that the incumbent in particular will be grateful to see churchwardens taking on is supervising the timing of an appeal and the associated works. We have already seen, in examining faculty jurisdiction, how vital it is to estimate the length of time each process can take when repairs or alterations are being planned. Raising the funds adds in a whole new dimension to the timetabling process, and it can at times seem immensely compli-cated, not to say circular. (To apply for a grant you may have to provide a specification with accurate costings from your preferred contractor, yet you are also advised not to go to tender until you have got the funds in place in case the contractor puts the price up between tendering and getting the go-ahead, and so on and so forth.) Someone with a clear head and an ability to write things down in a logical order – and it is to be hoped that these might be qualities belonging to at least one out of every two churchwar-dens! – can be worth their weight in gold.

A whole book could be written on just this one aspect of running a church in twenty-first-century Britain, so this is neces-sarily only a brief introduction to the pitfalls and challenges of fundraising; but it would be very surprising if this aspect of church life did not have to be tackled at some point during every six-year period of office.

Church security

The security of our churches and the property contained within them, for which the churchwardens are responsible, poses a major problem – one that, if not tackled, will see the money you manage to generate from your fundraising efforts pour out as fast as it comes in. If there has been no recent consultation with the crime-prevention officer (CPO) from the local police force, this should be one of the first items on a new churchwarden's list of things to do. Thefts from churches are increasing and, while they cannot be prevented entirely, the number can be reduced by taking appropriate precautions.

Furnishings and fittings are attractive to the thief; so also is the offertory box. A list distributed by the City of London Police details items that have been stolen from churches: vestry and sanctuary carpets (even threadbare ones); decorated wooden organ pipes; metal organ pipes; stained, patterned and even plain glass; locks complete with key handles and keys; hinges; doors; wooden carvings (not only figures but from the ends of pews); lecterns; parts of a pulpit and a font; stone statues; memorials of various sorts; paintings and pictures; musical instruments; vestments; stoles; altar cloths; lacework and (most popular of all) candlesticks; vases (with or without flowers); crosses and free-standing offertory boxes. At St Bartholomew the Great the rector's Bible has twice been stolen from his stall!

The churchwardens are responsible for the furnishings and ornaments in a very practical way and they should

- review practical aspects of security precautions, consulting the CPO, insurance company and other interested bodies;
- maintain contact with other neighbourhood groups committed to crime reduction;
- report any matters of note to the police and keep a record of all incidents;
- maintain contact with the insurance company.

It is, as we have seen, a legal requirement for the churchwardens to maintain an inventory of goods and ornaments. To be of use in preventing crime it must be quite detailed, containing accurate measurements of items together with a record of details, identifying marks, scratches, dents, etc. Items included in the inventory should also be photographed, not least so that the police can circulate a photograph of an item if it is stolen. Photographs may be taken by any keen photographer, one item at a time, against a neutral background, and with a ruler alongside the item to give an accurate scale. Photographs, negatives (or digital images) and an updated copy of the inventory should be kept in a safe place separate from the church building. Church property, like domestic property, can also be marked using ultraviolet markers. It is a deterrent to advertise that property is marked in this way.

Security begins with the exterior of the church building. In some areas simply making the building more visible will deter certain types of crime. Hedges can be pruned to a suitable height and security lighting, using photoelectric cells or movement detectors, can be used to make it easier to see people attempting to break into the church or its ancillary buildings. A simple CPO axiom is worth noting: criminals do not like to be bathed in light!

Climbing can be prevented by the use of anti-climb paint – the sort that does not dry and is very slippery – at not less than 3.1 m (8 ft) from the ground. Advertising the fact that drainpipes are coated acts as a deterrent. Roof materials can also be painted or coated with a bitumastic compound that will deter theft and make it more difficult to dispose of metal. Barbed wire, barbed tape and other devices can be fitted to low-level roofs to prevent access and deter criminals or vandals.

The CPO can advise you about locks. The lock on a large door must be suitable for the task; a simple domestic Yale lock is unlikely to be up to the job. A proper lock is nearly always larger than you think it is. The police recommend using just one door for the normal entrance and exit of visitors, thus reducing the criminal's opportunity for escape. You may well find a tension between the advice of the CPO and the recommendations of the local fire officer. The fire service advocates easily opened doors with crash bars to facilitate rapid exit, while the police suggest that all doors be kept locked and bolted unless it is absolutely necessary to open them. In a large building with many internal doors there are increased opportunities for an intruder to hide. Keypad locks can be a useful deterrent to the casual criminal and the codes can be changed regularly to prevent unauthorized access. They have the advantage of not requiring a key.

Key security is a very important aspect of overall security. In the Middle Ages the monks responsible for opening and closing the church, the sacristy, the kitchen and other doors were solemnly charged not to put their keys down or to leave them unattended.

The theft of a set of keys leaves you feeling very vulnerable, and changing locks can be very expensive.

The number of keyholders should be kept to a minimum and a register kept. It can sometimes be useful to have a double lock on the main entrance door with the second lock having keys held only by the minister and churchwardens. This makes it possible to prevent other keyholders entering the church when, for example, floor-cleaning or minor works are in progress of which not all keyholders may be aware. Ancillary buildings, including boiler-houses and sheds, need to be secured as well, especially if ladders or tools are stored in them.

Stained-glass windows present special opportunities for expensive damage. Depending on the degree of risk and the importance of the windows, consideration should be given to fitting a fine wire mesh or supplementary glazing in unbreakable materials. These and other fittings require faculties.

♦ 6 ♦

When problems arise

Examples of things going wrong, and how they might be resolved

We have already noted the balance that needs to be maintained among the three aspects of the office of churchwarden: responsibility to the bishop, collaboration with the incumbent and representation of the laity. This is not an easy balance to maintain and sometimes things can go wrong. Examples 6.1–6.3 illustrate how things might go wrong, with suggestions on how these situations, and ones like them, might be resolved.

EXAMPLE 6.1 Reporting the vicar's shortcomings

The problem
The churchwardens liked their vicar. He was pleasant, scholarly and rather bookish, and preferred to be at home with a book rather than visiting or out at social events. But he did not take much time over preparing services, rarely preached a comprehensible sermon and was so forgetful that he was late for a funeral and had gone away on the day of a wedding. The archdeacon's visitation was shortly due and they agonized over whether they were duty bound to tell him the facts.

A possible solution
These churchwardens like their vicar – which must be a good point from which to start. Clearly they do not want to get him into trouble, but they also recognize that they have a responsibility to the parish, and to the archdeacon and bishop, which they must not shirk.

The first thing they need to do is to speak to their vicar. They will want to make this a non-confrontational meeting, but they will also want to be firm and to the point. They should present themselves as people who want to help the vicar fulfil his ministry to the best of his ability; their criticism needs to be constructive and appreciative of the vicar's good points. They may want to begin by telling him how much they value his friendship and appreciate his learning, but, though they may find it embarrassing to do so, they need to go on to remind him of the problems his forgetfulness has caused; they also need to tell him that they have difficulty understanding his sermons and point out that if even they cannot understand them, it is likely that newcomers to the Christian faith have even more difficulty.

The churchwardens could then tell their vicar that they find themselves in an embarrassing position over the archdeacon's visitation, and that they do not wish to report his shortcomings, but that they need to see a significant improvement if they are to agree not to do so. Much now depends on the vicar's response. If he is able to admit that he does have some problems in the way he organizes his work, and some understanding that he is probably spending too much time alone with his books, then there is a way forward. Prior to the meeting, the churchwardens could have done some research on time-management courses and other in-service training offered by the diocese or other bodies, and they could stipulate that, if the vicar agrees to go on one of these courses, they will not this time report the problems to the archdeacon. They are in effect giving the vicar a year to sort himself out.

Realistically, however, it is unlikely that this bookish and absent-minded vicar will ever become a super-efficient extrovert. The churchwardens therefore also need to take account of the ingrained aspects of his personality and do what they can to compensate for them. They should probably arrange between themselves to phone him before an important event to try to make sure he has not forgotten about it. They might need to call at the vicarage, or get someone else reliable to do so, to ensure he arrives on time for the next funeral. With a bit of luck, he may get so sick of being treated like a baby that he manages to reform. On the other hand, he may not.

His disinclination for social events and visiting also needs to be handled in an encouraging way, and again this may require a greater time commitment from the churchwardens, at least for a limited period. Perhaps they could offer to go visiting with him, or find someone else prepared to do this. They could perhaps organize some small social gatherings – just a few congenial people for dinner – and invite the vicar, so that he can socialize without it feeling like a chore. Alternatively, or if such initiatives do not work out, they may decide to accept that he is just never going to undertake this side of parish life, but that they value him sufficiently for his strong points that they are prepared to delegate such activities to other members of the church. They may consider that no human being is ever going to fulfil all the criteria for the perfect vicar, but that he fulfils enough of them for it to be worth putting up with his lack of interest in the social arena.

Concerning his sermons, having once broached the subject of his incomprehensibility, it is important that the churchwardens continue to offer him feedback, thanking him when he has clearly taken the effort to prepare his sermons properly and asking questions to help him clarify his thoughts if necessary.

If, however, the vicar refuses to take on board any of the churchwardens' concerns over his performance, denies that there is any problem and refuses to come out of his study, then they will regretfully decide they must take the matter up with the archdeacon. They should, however, inform the vicar that this is what they are going to do, so that there is no sense of 'telling tales'.

EXAMPLE 6.2 Dealing with finances

The problem
The PCC was pleased with the accounts presented by the treasurer. They completely hid the bequest recently received and it could be put away for the rainy day when the church

roof might just start to leak. At the meeting with the rural dean and archdeacon to talk about the shortfall in payments to the Common Fund, the churchwardens were expected to plead poverty in the name of the parish and to keep the nest egg intact.

A possible solution

The churchwardens must be aware that they really cannot allow matters to proceed on this basis. It is their duty to ensure that the PCC fulfils its responsibilities and legal requirements and, as trustees of a charity excepted from registration, this includes accurate financial reporting.

To avoid embarrassing the treasurer, the churchwardens may wish to schedule a meeting alone with him or her to insist that financial reporting must be accurate and transparent and to make the necessary adjustments to the accounts. They should also ensure that their incumbent, as chair of the PCC, is kept fully informed of these developments and is involved in so far as he or she wishes to be. There then needs to be a further discussion with the PCC to determine, on the basis of genuine financial information, how the parish will meet its requirement to pay the agreed 'quota' and how it should respond to any request to increase that quota. To facilitate this, the churchwardens may be able to play for time a little in their meeting with the rural dean and archdeacon by stressing the need to go back to their PCC to present the concerns of the diocese – that is, they need not make a commitment to anything on behalf of the PCC at that meeting. But they do need to make the position very clear to the PCC and not allow it to 'hide' any of the church's resources.

This is not, of course, to say that the PCC should give all its money away, or fail to make responsible provision for the future. It is acceptable to hold a certain amount of money in reserve, worked out on the basis of what it would cost to keep the church running for, say, 30 weeks, if for some reason income completely dried up. But the reserves policy needs to be decided and recorded in the annual report.

The churchwardens could also point out to the PCC that

any fundraising initiatives will be hampered if the church is perceived to be, or suspected of, sitting on a large amount of money. Trusts that are approached for grants almost invariably want to see the most recent accounts and annual report, and the people who examine them are skilled at noting discrepancies and asking questions. If they think you are holding more money than you should be, they will not make a grant. Also, if your PCC and congregation begin to bask in the idea that there is money tucked away for a rainy day, they are themselves less likely either to respond to appeals or to increase their regular pledged giving.

There is another way forward that could be examined (though no archdeacon will thank us for suggesting this). You could consider setting up a separate charitable trust, whose aims are to support your church but which is run quite separately from it, as a registered charity with its own body of trustees. Donors could be encouraged, for certain projects or in certain circumstances (some donors will not give to 'religion', but they will give to 'heritage', for instance) to give to this body, rather than to the church. You would of course have to fulfil all the accounting and reporting requirements of registered charities for this new body, including filing the necessary reports with the Charity Commission, but this would not be money available to the diocese. If you decide to go down this path, you should seek specialist advice from a charity lawyer and/or the Charity Commission.

EXAMPLE 6.3 Motivating the PCC

The problem
The vicar and churchwardens of St Andrew's always got on well together. They had regular meetings, discussed plans and proposals before taking them to the standing committee and PCC, and also met socially. PCC members began to wonder if they had any role other than that of rubber-stamping decisions made in the pub by the vicar and churchwardens.

A possible solution

It is understandable that the vicar and churchwardens are resistant to what they may perceive as 'interference' from PCC members, when they feel that they are doing a good job, know how things work and are best left to get on with it. They are concerned that to involve PCC members more directly will take up time, time that could better be spent getting on with the job. This is, however, at best a short-term approach (the churchwardens will at some point need to be replaced, and how will anyone else have the experience to take on the job?) and, at worst, there is potential here for genuine discontent among PCC members, which could turn into opposition.

Churchwardens need to be aware of, and take seriously, 'rumblings' from PCC members. PCC members themselves need to make their views known to churchwardens. If, as may be the case here, they find that the churchwardens will not listen to them, or are dismissive, they can ask a member of the standing committee to raise their concerns at the next committee meeting.

It is true that involving PCC members in the work of running the church, rather than just attending meetings and dutifully voting 'yes', does take time – particularly when new members are voted on to the PCC and one has to go over old ground, revisiting issues that the vicar and churchwardens had hoped were closed – but it is part of the responsibility of the churchwardens to enable the PCC to be effective.

There are ways of solving this problem – or, rather, opportunity – without it taking up too much time, and one way is actually to give PCC members things to do, specific areas of responsibility. Keep them busy, in other words, so that in fact they have *less* time to sit around discussing the churchwardens' shortcomings, but are able to make a genuine contribution. One way of doing this is to set up PCC 'working parties' with a specific brief to handle a particular issue (drafting a child-protection policy document, for instance, or liaising with the director of music, improving communications with the bellringers, or organizing an event). Ensure that every PCC member joins at least one of these working parties, and also make it a requirement that the working parties report on their progress to each full PCC meeting. That way you lessen the risk of any small group of people falling out of line with the overall direction of the parish. You will by this means not only lessen discontent, but discover the talents and abilities of your PCC members and lighten the load of the churchwardens. And PCC meetings will become more business-like and balanced, in which the reporting will not be in one direction only.

The scenario in Example 6.4 is the kind that may be experienced by a new incumbent who succeeds an elderly priest with whom the churchwardens feel a continuing affinity, while Example 6.5 offers another scenario relating to a new incumbent. Some problems may appear, or even be, intractable, like that in Example 6.6.

EXAMPLE 6.4 A very different vicar

The problem
Gillian was the newly appointed vicar of three country parishes. She lived in the largest village, which would be the primary focus of her ministry. Her predecessor had retired at 70 but he was a man of boundless energy. He believed that the vicar should be useful, and had organized a luncheon club for the elderly, raised money for the village school, spent time with the cricket team and drunk in the pub. He was living in the nearby town. Gillian did not think that her prime job was to be useful; she placed an emphasis on prayer and worship, on spending time with people and listening to them, and she was quite happy for lay people to run the various village organizations. She tried out her ideas on the churchwardens. They were not very enthusiastic and they did not keep her confidence. They went straight to the retired vicar and told him what she was planning, and she was soon aware of his continued influence on the parish.

A possible solution

This is not an easy problem to solve, as the churchwardens have already made the fundamental mistake of breaking the new minister's confidence. They have not adopted the role she was expecting of them – that of being trusted sounding-boards on whom she should indeed be able to try out her ideas. They did not need to accept her ideas; they could have told her which ones they thought would not work, and why they would not. They, after all, know the parish far better than she can at this stage, and if she cannot try out her ideas on the churchwardens, then where can she turn for advice? And she was taking a sensible step in discussing them first, rather than just going ahead and implementing them.

There are bound to be changes of emphasis when a new vicar arrives, particularly when there is such a difference in outlook and age (and, yes, gender) from the previous incumbent. If these churchwardens really feel fundamentally opposed to what the new vicar wants to do, and are not prepared even to listen to her ideas, then they would do best to resign at the next APCM and let people more in tune with her take over. (These churchwardens, along with the other members of the PCC and congregation, may also have become rather lazy, expecting the vicar to do all the work.) It would nevertheless be a pity for the parish to lose all their accumulated knowledge, particularly as the vicar did make an effort to consult them.

If this were a survival guide for vicars rather than for churchwardens, then one might suggest that Gillian pay a visit to her predecessor and attempt to win his confidence and support. It is quite possible that the churchwardens have described her proposed changes in a more blunt way than she intends to introduce them, and it is also possible that the retired vicar has more wisdom and understanding of the need for change than the churchwardens have given him credit for.

Ideally, at least one of the churchwardens will now be feeling rather guilty at having broken Gillian's confidence, and will apologize and attempt to rebuild trust. It is important to remember that the right course is often worked out only after some rather wild ideas have been flung around. The new vicar needs churchwardens who are genuinely capable of responding to her ideas, who do not take fright at the thought of some things being done differently and who recognize that change is a necessary aspect of life and growth, but who are also able to give sound advice, drawing on their knowledge of what works in their parish. And while they may quite understandably wish to maintain their friendship with the previous vicar, they must remember that it is not now to him that their primary loyalty is owed, and they should avoid discussing parish matters with him.

EXAMPLE 6.5 Resenting the new vicar's authority

The problem
The new vicar found that the reader had been exercising most of the incumbent's functions during the interregnum. It might have been possible to resolve the issues of authority, but the reader was also opposed to the vicar's 'High Church ways' and expressed his views forcefully to his wife, who was the churchwarden.

A possible solution
Another difficult problem. This may be one that has to come to a head with some confrontation, and the vicar may want to consult the area dean and archdeacon sooner rather than later. It will need to be made clear to the reader that the vicar is now in charge, and that if he cannot accept the vicar's authority he will have to relinquish his position as reader in that parish.

Much will now depend on the character of the reader's wife, who does of course find herself in a difficult position. She may decide that the best option is to resign as churchwarden, doing so as amicably as possible and handing over to someone who does not face her divided loyalties. Or she may have sufficient influence on her husband to suggest that he give the new vicar a chance and stop moaning. One cannot help thinking that that is rather unlikely.

EXAMPLE 6.6 Discordant notes

The problem
The parish of St Nathaniel's had a strong musical tradition, and had been valued for many years for its commitment to formal choral worship. The previous incumbent having run away with the organist, a new rector was appointed, who in turn appointed a new organist – who turned out not to be up to the job. The quality of music in the services deteriorated rapidly, but the new rector had cloth ears and was completely oblivious to the problem. One of the churchwardens, a competent musician himself, kept trying to raise the problem with the rector, who obstinately repeated the Canons of the Church of England, stating that he alone had responsibility for the music and it was no one else's business. Meanwhile the number on the electoral roll went inexorably downwards.

A possible solution
Get someone to run away with the new organist!

How to pace yourself and take time off (as well as ensuring others do)

One of the challenges for officers of any voluntary organization, including the church, is what can be termed 'boundary maintenance'. It can be very difficult to know when to stop: there is always more work that could be done and never enough time to do it in, and finding other volunteers to help is not always easy. If churchwardens try to do everything and never give themselves time off, then resentment can set in. What began as a genuine desire to give the best of oneself to the fulfilling of the office can begin to feel like a burden; there can be a sense that people are taking you for granted and that you are the constant recipient of complaints and never of praise, and you find you cannot wait for your period of office to end. You may also begin to feel that the work you are actually paid to do – your employment or career – is suffering because of the time you are being forced to devote to the church; your family may be complaining that you do not give sufficient time to them; you may feel you have just had enough.

It is important to be aware, even in the first flush of enthusiasm after your initial appointment as a churchwarden, that these difficulties may arise if you do not plan for them. So the first thing to do is remember that there are two of you. Sit down with your fellow churchwarden and plan your division of labour. You do not need to be at every service or every event of your church. For the most important services and events, you will both want to be there. You are likely to know well in advance when these are; you can warn your family that you will be at church and plan your other commitments around these times. You will also be aware of busy times of year: the run-up to the APCM, for instance, when you will be involved in preparing the annual report, and, to a lesser extent, the preparation time for each PCC meeting. But on a Sunday by Sunday basis, you may decide that one churchwarden will be in regular attendance at a morning service with the other present in the evening. And 'regular' does not have to mean 'every single Sunday without fail'. The important thing is to communicate with your fellow churchwarden and the incumbent, so that you are known to be reliable. If you say you are going to be at church, then be there, but do not over-commit yourself.

Your presence at church or at church-related events is only a part of your commitment, of course. You will also be one of the first points of contact for anyone wishing to raise issues about the church – in other words, your phone may ring a lot. If you have not done so already, make sure either that you have an answering machine or that you have set up the answering service offered by your phone company. You will need to strike a balance here, so that you are available when needed but are not constantly at risk of being interrupted or finding that all your evenings are taken up with what can degenerate into gossipy, time-wasting discussions about church matters. You may find it useful to subscribe to a caller-display service on your land line (if you have a mobile phone you can programme it yourself to tell you who is calling). You are likely to want to answer straightaway if it is your fellow churchwarden or your minister calling, and you will certainly want to respond at once if it is the security firm telling you the church burglar alarm has just gone off; but you may decide that the PCC member who is calling you for the third time this evening about some minor matter can leave a message to which you will respond at a more convenient moment.

It is always tempting, never more so than in the church, to regard oneself as indispensable, to take the easy if more time-consuming option that says, 'If you want something doing, do it yourself'. Delegation is a skill that has to be learnt, but enabling others to undertake tasks, rather than trying to undertake them all oneself, is an important aspect of a senior office in any organization and to do this well may be one of the longest-lasting benefits you can bring to your church. Use your PCC members; do not allow them to think they are just there to have nice long discussions while you and the incumbent do all the work. Look out for other people who want to help in some way and give them the opportunity to do so. To build up a team of people able and willing to undertake various aspects of church organization will take pressure off you, assist in building up a sense of fellowship and belonging, and help identify future potential churchwardens. Think of yourself as an 'enabler', not only as a 'doer'. It can take time and effort to train other people, but is always worth it.

Everything that has been said above – about your need to take time off, to pace yourself, not to be on call 24 hours a day, seven days a week – can be applied with equal force to your incumbent, who is probably under even greater pressure than you to work round the clock. Understanding your own need for boundary maintenance should assist you in ensuring that your minister is supported in managing his or her own boundaries. Depending on the personality and work patterns of your minister, you may at times need to be forceful in insisting that he or she takes time off. You may need to deflect a member of the congregation who wants to tackle the minister on some minor but controversial issue at the end of an exhausting Sunday. In this, as in your own dealings with people, you will need to discriminate between what is really urgent and what can wait.

There can be a tendency, among both church and non-church people, to imagine that Christians must always be ready to respond to any expressed need, no matter how trivial or even mischievous, and to do so with never a cross word, never appearing to be tired, and always with a loving smile. There can even be a tendency to expect this of yourself, which is likely to mean that you have a constant sense of failure. It is important to remember that even Jesus could become tired and that after hours of healing, preaching and dealing with people's problems he too felt the need to escape – in search of solitude, prayer and restoration of body and spirit. St Mark relates[10] how the disciples came to search him out, saying, 'Where have you got to? Everyone's looking for you!' So when you need it, give yourself a break. Schedule it, tell people that's what you are doing – and do not let anyone make you feel guilty about it. And tell your minister to do the same.

If you have to go

Sometimes a churchwarden finds that he or she is incapable of discharging the duties of the office: this incapacity may be caused by job or family pressures, by ill health or by the need to move house. Sometimes a churchwarden finds that he or she cannot with integrity continue in the office, either because of some personal dilemma or because of profound disagreement on some crucial matter. If at all possible, the churchwarden should wait until the next meeting for the election of churchwardens and simply decline to accept nomination, but there are ways of vacating the office earlier. Such a decision to resign does not necessarily imply failure; indeed, 'failure' might be better defined as trying to carry on regardless of intolerable pressures or fundamental disagreements. Among the many ex-churchwardens who cannot even face going to church services, let alone sitting on the PCC, there must be plenty who carried on beyond the call of duty, becoming bitter when they would have done better to grasp the nettle and resign, whatever the temporary embarrassment.

One of the motives for writing this book was the hope that, if churchwardens had a better understanding of their office, fewer of them would end up alienated from the church they had served. As a churchwarden you have held an important office and been respected for your discharge of it. Your sudden departure or disappearance can have a demoralizing effect on the parish, which is why we urge churchwardens not to resign unless it is absolutely essential, and then not in a huff. If you really, really must go and do not want to join in worship at the church where you used to be churchwarden, then go and find another church. Look in the next deanery, if it is not too far away, find a service that suits you, and do not tell anyone you used to be a churchwarden. Never speak ill of the church you left. Let the experience of worship restore your joy in believing.

The best ways of leaving office, and the best time to do so

The simplest but not the best way to give up the office of church-warden is to render oneself ineligible for it. Anyone signifying to the parish electoral-roll officer a desire to have his or her name removed from the roll is no longer qualified to be a churchwarden, and the office must be vacated.

The correct way to resign is to give written notice to the bishop *by post* (not by telephone, fax or email). The resignation takes effect either two months after notice has been given or at an earlier date agreed by the bishop after consultation with the minister and any other churchwarden of the parish. (This is, incidentally, a simplification of the previous rules on resignation, which required a churchwarden wishing to resign to have the written consent of the minister and the other churchwarden before giving written notice to the bishop. Once the bishop accepted the resignation, the office was vacated forthwith.)

The best way to leave office, as mentioned earlier, is simply to come to the end of one's term and not seek re-election. And, in a contested election, you might find you are not re-elected anyway. Finally, after six consecutive years in office, you will not be eligible to seek re-election.

Whatever the circumstances, the churchwarden must hand over the office, rendering an account of all that he or she has done. In particular, the terrier, inventory and log-book are to be passed over and checked by his or her successor. Any property belonging to the church must be returned and any moneys – petty cash, for example – repaid.

As an ex-churchwarden, your experience counts for a great deal and you can still serve the church on the PCC or in other ways. When people see that a person who has occupied the parish's highest lay office is prepared to return to the pews, to join the church cleaning team, to be an acolyte, to help out at the Christmas fair, then it reinforces the important teaching about ministry of all sorts as humble service and encourages others to offer their own skills, talents and time. And, with your wealth of experience, you can be the one to propose at the APCM that thanks be returned to the minister and churchwardens for what they do, while knowing that they do not do it in order to be thanked.

Conclusion

Having read this, do I still want to be a churchwarden?

The office of churchwarden is only one of a number of possibilities that the Church of England provides for lay ministry. To know whether this is the right form of ministry for you, you must look at your gifts and strengths, the qualities you have and the time you have available, and you should also look at other forms of ministry – sidesmen, vergers, servers, singers, assistant ministers of Holy Communion, parish visitors, children's workers, readers, and others developed in different dioceses and parishes. If your gifts seem particularly suited for the role of churchwarden and if you are willing to approach the office in a spirit of service, then you should offer yourself for election.

Do I have the right qualities to be a churchwarden?

As we have already seen, the task of a churchwarden is threefold. The churchwarden is the leading representative of the laity, works closely with the minister, and is also an officer of the bishop. The question is often asked of a minister when he or she puts forward an idea to the bishop or archdeacon: 'What do the churchwardens think?'

A churchwarden needs to command the respect of the minister, the PCC and the congregation, to be available for consultation, to be willing to make decisions in collaboration with others and to carry them through, to be ready to listen, to be a skilled communicator and to facilitate communication between others.

It should also be clear by now what reasons there are for *not* seeking to become a churchwarden. The office is not about feeling important and walking up and down with a wand. In particular, seeking the office purely in order to be a thorn in the flesh for the minister is not a good motive. There has always been a recognition in the Church that the minister and one or other of the churchwardens might not get on together. Sometimes a new minister finds the existing churchwardens are hostile to him or her and opposed to what he or she wants to do in the parish. Clearly the minister will not want that person to be churchwarden for a subsequent term.

If, after reading this book, you are feeling challenged and inspired, rather than depressed, then you may well possess the qualities to make a good churchwarden.

Do I have the time?

You should have a fairly clear idea by now of the likely time commitment involved. To be effective, a churchwarden needs to devote quite a lot of time to the job, becoming conversant with the main areas of responsibility as well as being prepared to get to know the congregation that has elected him or her to office. Time must be a factor in reaching your decision; if you cannot afford to give the time, do not accept the office.

You will need to be a regular attender at church so that you become a familiar face. It is slightly easier if your parish church has only morning services, but if it also has a well-attended evening service you need to be seen there as well. This does not mean that a churchwarden must go to everything, but he or she represents the 8-o'clock and Evensong congregations as well as the Parish Eucharist congregation, the Tuesday morning Communion group as well as the Thursday Bible class. A churchwarden needs to know what is going on and who the regular members of each congregation are. You also cannot be a churchwarden if you expect to be away every year at Christmas or Easter!

Should I offer or wait to be asked?

So then, you are qualified, realize the commitment involved, and think you would do a reasonably good job as a churchwarden; what should you do next? It has never been quite clear how the candidates for churchwarden emerge, but it is certainly the case that there is rarely a stampede for office. Anyone who is qualified and can find a nominator and seconder can stand for election; no one has to wait to be asked. It would still be sensible, however, to declare an interest in being churchwarden early on and to discuss it with the incumbent and with the existing wardens. It is also always worth serving an apprenticeship on the PCC and deanery synod in order to come to an understanding of the way in which decisions are made and implemented in the Church. A churchwarden-in-waiting, and willing to wait, can be very useful, especially when illness, sudden death, the demands of a job or some other matter unexpectedly leads to vacation of office.

An office 'worthy of all honour'

By now you should have a clear understanding of both the burdens and the rewards implicit in paragraph 4 of Canon E.1 of the Canons of the Church of England, headed 'Of churchwardens':

The churchwardens when admitted are officers of the Ordinary. They shall discharge such duties as are by law and custom assigned to them; they shall be foremost in representing the laity and in co-operating with the incumbent; they shall use their best endeavours by example and precept to encourage the parishioners in the practice of true religion and to promote unity and peace among them. They shall also maintain order and decency in the church and churchyard, especially during the time of divine service.

You will also have an understanding of how the office of churchwarden has evolved over the centuries and some vision of how it might function today. You will know what are the practical tasks you are called upon to perform and you will be looking forward to encouraging 'the parishioners in the practice of true religion'.

You are likely to have been struck by the predominance of 'complaints' in the role of the churchwarden. Churchwardens have always been expected to 'make complaint' against the minister when necessary, and to some extent we have continued this emphasis with our recommendation that PCCs draw up and agree a complaints procedure. It is an undoubted fact of church life that churchwardens, quite apart from their own official duty to complain, will find themselves the recipients of the complaints of others.

Churchwardens have a vital part to play here in not exacerbating this 'culture of complaint', in not allowing what are frequently minor disagreements and quibbles to build up into major issues. They need to pray for the gifts of wisdom, forbearance and understanding in responding to the needs of both the congregation and the minister. Sometimes all that a complainant needs is a listening ear – having 'sounded off' about the flowers, the music, the sermon or the incense, the complainant may already feel better and go away comforted. Churchwardens need to be able to distinguish between the normal human desire for a bit of a moan, the more troublesome constant low-level grumbling that can be a drain on everyone's energy, and the genuine concern that needs to be addressed. They also need to strike a balance between conveying every petty grievance to the minister and failing to keep him or her informed on potentially important issues as they arise.

In dealing with trivial complaints and purely gossipy comments, they should not be afraid to discourage the moaner or gossiper from continuing in this vein. Likewise, when something the minister is saying or doing is likely, in their judgement, to lead to division and difficulties within the church, the churchwardens must not be afraid to warn the minister. The golden rule here is to avoid a public confrontation between churchwardens and minister. If the minister knows that he or she can rely on the absolute confidence and discretion of the churchwardens and on their support in front of others, then he or she is far more likely to take note of disagreements and cautions expressed by the churchwardens in private.

In all these personal relations, the aim of the churchwardens should indeed be 'to promote unity and peace', remembering, as Archdeacon Delaney pointed out in his 2001 visitation charge, that we 'are all in it together'.

In striving to achieve this aim, it is vital that churchwardens do not neglect their own spiritual life. It can be very difficult for those of us involved in the conduct and running of church services to find them occasions for true devotion – we can be too anxious, and too busy making sure that everyone else is happy and knows what they are doing. It is doubly important, therefore, that time is set aside for private prayer, reading of the Scriptures and prayerful reflection on the work to be done.

Nobody is perfect, whether minister, congregation or church-warden. In undertaking this office, it is important to be able to forgive others, and oneself, and, after something has not gone quite according to plan, to let it go, to resolve to do better next time, and to carry on. Most of the time, it is to be hoped, you will be rewarded by the awareness of the privilege of taking part in the mission of the Church to bring about God's kingdom on earth; and, at the end of your term of office, when you come to hand over the inventory, the log-book and the account of your work, you will be able to say with thanksgiving and sincerity, as our Lord instructed his disciples to say: 'We are unprofitable servants: we have done that which was our duty to do.'[11]

Appendix 1

Parochial Church Councils (Powers) Measure 1956

1 Definitions
In this Measure –
'Council' means a parochial church council;
'Diocesan Authority' means the Diocesan Board of Finance or any existing or future body appointed by the Diocesan Synod to act as trustees of diocesan trust property;
'Minister' and 'Parish' have the meanings respectively assigned to them in the Rules for the Representation of the Laity.

2 General functions of council
   (1) It shall be the duty of the minister and the parochial church council to consult together on matters of general concern and importance to the parish.

   (2) The functions of parochial church councils shall include –
(a) co-operation with the minister in promoting in the parish the whole mission of the Church, pastoral, evangelistic, social and ecumenical;
(b) the consideration and discussions of matters concerning the Church of England or any other matters of religious or public interest, but not the declaration of the doctrine of the Church on any question;
(c) making known and putting into effect any provision made by the diocesan synod or the deanery synod, but without prejudice to the powers of the council on any particular matter;
(d) giving advice to the diocesan synod and the deanery synod on any matter referred to the council;
(e) raising such matters as the council consider appropriate with the diocesan synod or deanery synod.

(3) In the exercise of its functions the parochial church council shall take into consideration any expression of opinion by any parochial church meeting.

3 Council to be a body corporate

Every council shall be a body corporate by the name of the parochial church council of the parish for which it is appointed and shall have perpetual succession. Any act of the council may be signified by an instrument executed pursuant to a resolution of the council and under the hands or if an instrument under seal is required under the hands and seals of the chairman presiding and two other members of the council present at the meeting at which such resolution is passed.

7 Miscellaneous powers of council

The council of every parish shall have the following powers in addition to any powers conferred by the Constitution or otherwise by this Measure –

(i) Power to frame an annual budget of moneys required for the maintenance of the work of the Church in the parish and otherwise and to take such steps as they think necessary for the raising, collecting and allocating of such moneys;

(ii) Power to make levy and collect a voluntary church rate for any purpose connected with the affairs of the church including the administrative expenses of the council and the costs of any legal proceedings;

(iii) Power jointly with the minister to appoint and dismiss the parish clerk and sexton or any persons performing or assisting to perform the duties of parish clerk or sexton and to determine their salaries and the conditions of the tenure of their offices or of their employment but subject to the rights of any persons holding the said offices at the appointed day;

(iv) Power jointly with the minister to determine the objects to which all moneys to be given or collected in church shall be allocated;

(v) Power to make representations to the bishop with regard to any matter affecting the welfare of the church in the parish.

Appendix 2

Care of Churches and Ecclesiastical Jurisdiction Measure 1991 (No. 1)

Duties of churchwardens as to recording of information about churches

4. (1) In every parish it shall be the duty of the churchwardens –
(a) to compile and maintain –
  (i) a full terrier of all lands appertaining to the church;
  (ii) a full inventory of all articles appertaining to the church;
(b) to insert in a log-book maintained for the purpose a full note of all alterations, additions and repairs to, and other events affecting, the church and the lands and articles appertaining thereto and of the location of any other documents relating to such alterations, additions, repairs and events which are not kept with the log-book.

(2) In carrying out their duty under subsection (1) above the churchwardens shall act in consultation with the minister.

(3) The form of the terrier, inventory and log-book shall accord with such recommendations as the Council for the Care of Churches may make.

(4) The churchwardens shall send a copy of the inventory to such person as the bishop of the diocese concerned may designate from time to time for the purpose of this subsection as soon as practicable after it is compiled and shall notify that person of any alterations at such intervals as the bishop may direct from time to time.

(5) This section applies in relation to each church in a parish containing more than one church.

Duties of churchwardens as to fabric etc. of churches
5. (1) In every parish it shall be the duty of the churchwardens –
(a) at least once in every year, to inspect or cause an inspection to be made of the fabric of the church and all articles appertaining to the church;
(b) in every year, to deliver to the parochial church council and on behalf of that council to the annual parochial church meeting a report (referred to below as 'the annual fabric report') on the fabric of the church and all articles appertaining to the church, having regard to the inspection or inspections carried out under paragraph (a) above, including an account of all actions taken or proposed during the previous year for their protection and maintenance and, in particular, for the implementation of any recommendation contained in a report under a scheme made in pursuance of section 1 of the Inspection of Churches Measure 1955.

(2) In carrying out their duty under subsection (1) above the churchwardens shall act in consultation with the minister.

(3) The annual fabric report shall be delivered to the parochial church council at its meeting next before the annual parochial church meeting and, with such amendments as that council may make, to the ensuing annual parochial church meeting.

(4) The churchwardens shall, as soon as practicable after the beginning of each year, produce to the parochial church council the terrier, the inventory and the log-book relating to events occurring in the previous year and such other records as they consider likely to assist the council in discharging its functions in relation to the fabric of the church and articles appertaining to the church.

(5) Any terrier, inventory or log-book produced to the parochial church council in accordance with subsection (4) above shall be accompanied by a statement, signed by the churchwardens, to the effect that the contents thereof are accurate.

(6) This section applies in relation to each church in a parish containing more than one church.

(7) In this section 'year' means calendar year.

© Crown Copyright 1991

Appendix 3

Charities Act 1993
(as amended by the Charities Act 2006)

Persons disqualified from being trustees of a charity.

72. (1) Subject to the following provisions of this section, a person shall be disqualified for being a charity trustee or trustee for a charity if –

(a) he has been convicted of any offence involving dishonesty or deception;

(b) he has been adjudged bankrupt or sequestration of his estate has been awarded and (in either case) he has not been discharged;

(c) he has made a composition or arrangement with, or granted a trust deed for, his creditors and has not been discharged in respect of it;

(d) he has been removed from the office of charity trustee or trustee for a charity by an order made –

   (i)   by the Commissioners under section 18(2)(i) above, or

  (ii) by the Commissioners under section 20(1A)(i) of the Charities Act 1960 (power to act for protection of charities) or under section 20(1)(i) of that Act (as in force before the commencement of section 8 of the Charities Act 1992), or

 (iii) by the High Court,

on the grounds of any misconduct or mismanagement in the administration of the charity for which he was responsible or to which he was privy, or which he by his conduct contributed to or facilitated;

(e) he has been removed, under section 7 of the Law Reform (Miscellaneous Provisions) (Scotland) Act 1990 (powers of Court of Session to deal with management of charities), from being concerned in the management or control of any body;

(f) he is subject to a disqualification order under the Company

Directors Disqualification Act 1986 or to an order made under section 429(2)(b) of the Insolvency Act 1986 (failure to pay under county court administration order).

(2) In subsection (1) above –
(a) paragraph (a) applies whether the conviction occurred before or after the commencement of that subsection, but does not apply in relation to any conviction which is a spent conviction for the purposes of the Rehabilitation of Offenders Act 1974;
(b) paragraph (b) applies whether the adjudication of bankruptcy or the sequestration occurred before or after the commencement of that subsection;
(c) paragraph (c) applies whether the composition or arrangement was made, or the trust deed was granted, before or after the commencement of that subsection; and
(d) paragraphs (d) to (f) apply in relation to orders made and removals effected before or after the commencement of that subsection.

(3) Where (apart from this subsection) a person is disqualified under subsection (1)(b) above for being a charity trustee or trustee for any charity which is a company, he shall not be so disqualified if leave has been granted under section 11 of the Company Directors Disqualification Act 1986 (undischarged bankrupts) for him to act as director of the charity; and similarly a person shall not be disqualified under subsection (1)(f) above for being a charity trustee or trustee for such a charity if –
(a) in the case of a person subject to a disqualification order, leave under the order has been granted for him to act as director of the charity, or
(b) in the case of a person subject to an order under section 429(2)(b) of the Insolvency Act 1986, leave has been granted by the court which made the order for him to so act.

(4) The Commissioners may, on the application of any person disqualified under subsection (1) above, waive his disqualification either generally or in relation to a particular charity or a particular class of charities; but no such waiver may be granted in relation to any charity which is a company if –

(a) the person concerned is for the time being prohibited, by virtue of –

  (i) a disqualification order under the Company Directors Disqualification Act 1986, or

  (ii) section 11(1) or 12(2) of that Act (undischarged bankrupts; failure to pay under county court administration order), from acting as director of the charity; and

(b) leave has not been granted for him to act as director of any other company.

  (4A) If—

(a) a person disqualified under subsection (1)(d) or (e) makes an application under subsection (4) above five years or more after the date on which his disqualification took effect, and

(b) the Commission is not prevented from granting the application by virtue of paragraphs (a) and (b) of subsection (4),

the Commission must grant the application unless satisfied that, by reason of any special circumstances, it should be refused.

  (5) Any waiver under subsection (4) above shall be notified in writing to the person concerned.

  (6) For the purposes of this section the Commissioners shall keep, in such manner as they think fit, a register of all persons who have been removed from office as mentioned in subsection (1)(d) above either –

(a) by an order of the Commissioners made before or after the commencement of subsection (1) above, or

(b) by an order of the High Court made after the commencement of section 45(1) of the Charities Act 1992;

and, where any person is so removed from office by an order of the High Court, the court shall notify the Commissioners of his removal.

  (7) The entries in the register kept under subsection (6) above shall be available for public inspection in legible form at all reasonable times.

Appendix 4

Churchwardens Measure 2001
2001 No. 1

A Measure passed by the General Synod of the Church of England to make fresh provision with respect to churchwardens in the Church of England.

[10th April 2001]

1 Number and qualifications of churchwardens
(1) Subject to the provisions of this Measure there shall be two churchwardens of every parish.

(2)
(a) Where by virtue of a designation made by a pastoral scheme or otherwise a parish has more than one parish church, two church-wardens shall be appointed for each of the parish churches, and this Measure shall apply separately to each pair of churchwardens, but all the churchwardens shall be churchwardens of the whole parish except so far as they may arrange to perform separate duties in relation to the several parish churches.
(b) A church building or part of a building designated as a parish centre of worship under section 29(2) of the Pastoral Measure 1983 (1983 No. 1) shall, subject to subsection (4) of that section, be deemed while the designation is in force to be a parish church for the purposes of this subsection.

(3) The churchwardens of every parish shall be chosen from persons who have been baptised and –
(a) whose names are on the church electoral roll of the parish;
(b) who are actual communicants;
(c) who are twenty-one years of age or upwards; and
(d) who are not disqualified under section 2 or 3 below.

(4) If it appears to the bishop, in the case of any particular person who is not qualified by virtue of paragraph (a), (b) or (c) of subsection (3) above, that there are exceptional circumstances which justify a departure from the requirements of those paragraphs the bishop may permit that person to hold the office of churchwarden notwithstanding that those requirements are not met. Any such permission shall apply only to the period of office next following the date on which the permission is given.

(5) No person shall be chosen as churchwarden of a parish for any period of office unless he –
(a) has signified consent to serve as such; and
(b) has not signified consent to serve as such for the same period of office in any other parish (not being a related parish) or, if such consent has been signified and the meeting of the parishioners to elect churchwardens of that other parish has been held, was not chosen as churchwarden of that other parish.

In this subsection 'related parish' means a parish –
(a) belonging to the benefice to which the first-mentioned parish belongs; or
(b) belonging to a benefice held in plurality with the benefice to which the first-mentioned parish belongs; or
(c) having the same minister as the first-mentioned parish.

(6) In relation to the filling of a casual vacancy among the churchwardens the reference in subsection (5)(b) above to the same period of office shall be construed as a reference to a period of office which includes the period for which the casual vacancy is to be filled.

2 General disqualifications

(1) A person shall be disqualified from being chosen for the office of churchwarden if he is disqualified from being a charity trustee under section 72(1) of the Charities Act 1993 (c. 10) and the disqualification is not for the time being subject to a general waiver by the Charity Commissioners under subsection (4) of that section or to a waiver by them under that subsection in respect of all ecclesiastical charities established for purposes relating to the parish concerned.

In this subsection 'ecclesiastical charity' has the same meaning as that assigned to that expression in the Local Government Act 1894 (c. 73).

(2)
(a) A person shall be disqualified from being chosen for the office of churchwarden if he has been convicted of any offence mentioned in Schedule 1 to the Children and Young Persons Act 1933 (c. 12).
(b) In paragraph (a) above the reference to any offence mentioned in Schedule 1 to the Children and Young Persons Act 1933 shall include an offence which, by virtue of any enactment, is to be treated as being included in any such reference in all or any of the provisions of that Act.

(3) A person shall be disqualified from being chosen for the office of churchwarden if he is disqualified from holding that office under section 10(6) of the Incumbents (Vacation of Benefices) Measure 1977 (No. 1).

(4) All rules of law whereby certain persons are disqualified from being chosen for the office of churchwarden shall cease to have effect.

3 Disqualification after six periods of office
Without prejudice to section 2 above, a person shall be disqualified from being chosen for the office of churchwarden when that person has served as a churchwarden of the same parish for six successive periods of office until the annual meeting of the parishioners to elect churchwardens in the next year but one following the date on which that person vacated office at the end of the last such period:

Provided that a meeting of the parishioners may by resolution decide that this section shall not apply in relation to the parish concerned.

Any such resolution may be revoked by a subsequent meeting of the parishioners.

4 Time and manner of choosing

(1) The churchwardens of a parish shall be chosen annually not later than the 30th April in each year.

(2) Subject to the provisions of this Measure the churchwardens of a parish shall be elected by a meeting of the parishioners.

(3) Candidates for election at the meeting must be nominated and seconded in writing by persons entitled to attend the meeting and each nomination paper must include a statement, signed by the person nominated, to the effect that that person is willing to serve as a churchwarden and is not disqualified under section 2(1), (2) or (3) above.

(4) A nomination shall not be valid unless –
(a) the nomination paper is received by the minister of the parish before the commencement of the meeting; and
(b) in the case of a person who is not qualified by virtue of section 1(3) (a), (b) or (c) above, the bishop's permission was given under section 1(4) above before the nomination paper is received by the minister of the parish.

(5) If it appears to the minister of the parish that the election of any particular person nominated might give rise to serious difficulties between the minister and that person in the carrying out of their respective functions the minister may, before the election is conducted, make a statement to the effect that only one churchwarden is to be elected by the meeting. In that event one churchwarden shall be appointed by the minister from among the persons nominated, the name of the person so appointed being announced before the election is conducted, and the other shall then be elected by the meeting.

(6) During any period when there is no minister –
(a) subsection (4) above shall apply with the substitution for the words 'minister of the parish' of the words 'churchwarden by whom the notice convening the meeting was signed'; and
(b) subsection (5) above shall not apply.

(7) A person may be chosen to fill a casual vacancy among the churchwardens at any time.

(8) Any person chosen to fill a casual vacancy shall be chosen in the same manner as was the churchwarden whose place he is to fill except that, where the churchwarden concerned was appointed by the minister and the minister has ceased to hold office, the new churchwarden to fill the casual vacancy shall be elected by a meeting of the parishioners.

5 Meeting of the parishioners

(1) A joint meeting of –
(a) the persons whose names are entered on the church electoral roll of the parish; and
(b) the persons resident in the parish whose names are entered on a register of local government electors by reason of such residence,

shall be deemed to be a meeting of the parishioners for the purposes of this Measure.

(2) The meeting of the parishioners shall be convened by the minister or, during any period when there is no minister or when the minister is unable or unwilling to do so, the churchwardens of the parish by a notice signed by the minister or a churchwarden as the case may be.

(3) The notice shall state the place, day and hour at which the meeting of the parishioners is to be held.

(4) The notice shall be affixed on or near to the principal door of the parish church and of every other building licensed for public worship in the parish for a period including the last two Sundays before the meeting.

(5) The minister, if present, or, if he is not present, a chairman chosen by the meeting of the parishioners, shall preside thereat.

(6) In case of an equal division of votes on any question other than one to determine an election of a churchwarden the chairman

of the meeting of parishioners shall not have a second or casting vote and the motion on that question shall be treated as lost.

(7) The meeting of the parishioners shall have power to adjourn, and to determine its own rules of procedure.

(8) A person appointed by the meeting of the parishioners shall act as clerk of the meeting and shall record the minutes thereof.

6 Admission

(1) At a time and place to be appointed by the bishop annually, being on a date not later than 31st July in each year, each person chosen for the office of churchwarden shall appear before the bishop or his substitute duly appointed, and be admitted to the office of churchwarden after –

(a) making a declaration, in the presence of the bishop or his substitute, that he will faithfully and diligently perform the duties of his office; and

(b) subscribing a declaration to that effect and also that he is not disqualified under section 2(1), (2) or (3) above.

No person chosen for the office of churchwarden shall become churchwarden until such time as he shall have been admitted to office in accordance with the provisions of this section.

(2) Subject to the provisions of this Measure the term of office of the churchwardens so chosen and admitted as aforesaid shall continue until a date determined as follows, that is to say –

(a) in the case of a person who is chosen again as churchwarden at the next annual meeting of the parishioners –

    (i) if so admitted for the next term of office by 31st July in the year in question, the date of the admission; or

    (ii) if not so admitted for the next term of office by 31st July in the year in question, that date;

(b) in the case of a person who is not chosen again as churchwarden at the next annual meeting of the parishioners –

    (i) if that person's successor in office is so admitted for the next term of office by 31st July in the year in question, the date of the admission; or

(ii) if that person's successor in office is not so admitted for the next term of office by 31st July in the year in question, that date.

In the application of paragraph (b) above to any person, where there is doubt as to which of the new churchwardens is that person's successor in office the bishop may designate one of the new churchwardens as that person's successor for the purposes of that paragraph.

(3) Where any person ceases to hold the office of churchwarden at the end of July in any year by virtue of paragraph (a)(ii) or (b)(ii) above a casual vacancy in that office shall be deemed to have arisen.

(4) In relation to the filling of a casual vacancy the reference in subsection (1) above to the 31st July shall be construed as a reference to a date three months after the person who is to fill the vacancy is chosen or the date of the next annual meeting of the parishioners to elect churchwardens, whichever is the earlier.

7 Resignation
(1) A person may resign the office of churchwarden in accordance with the following provisions of this section, but not otherwise.

(2) Written notice of intention to resign shall be served on the bishop by post.

(3) The resignation shall have effect and the office shall be vacated –
(a) at the end of the period of two months following service of the notice on the bishop; or
(b) on such earlier date as may be determined by the bishop after consultation with the minister and any other churchwarden of the parish.

8 Vacation of office
(1) The office of churchwarden of a parish shall be vacated if –
(a) the name of the person concerned is removed from the church

electoral roll of the parish under rule 1 of the Church Representation Rules; or

(b) the name of the person concerned is not on a new church electoral roll of the parish prepared under rule 2(4) of those Rules; or

(c) the churchwarden becomes disqualified under section 2(1), (2) or (3) above.

(2) For the purposes of this section a person who has been chosen for the office of churchwarden but has not yet been admitted to that office shall be deemed to hold that office, and the expressions 'office' and 'churchwarden' shall be construed accordingly.

9 Guild Churches

(1) In the case of every church in the City of London designated and established as a Guild Church under the City of London (Guild Churches) Acts 1952 and 1960 the churchwardens shall, notwithstanding anything to the contrary contained in those Acts, be actual communicant members of the Church of England except where the bishop shall otherwise permit.

(2) Subject to subsection (1) above, nothing in this Measure shall apply to the churchwardens of any church designated and established as a Guild Church under the City of London (Guild Churches) Acts 1952 and 1960.

(3) In this section 'actual communicant member of the Church of England' means a member of the Church of England who is confirmed or ready and desirous of being confirmed and has received Communion according to the use of the Church of England or of a church in communion with the Church of England at least three times during the twelve months preceding the date of his election or appointment.

10 Special provisions

(1) In the carrying out of the provisions of this Measure the bishop shall have power –

(a) to make provision for any matter not herein provided for;

(b) to appoint a person to do any act in respect of which there has been any neglect or default on the part of any person or body charged with any duty under this Measure;

(c) so far as may be necessary for the purpose of giving effect to the intentions of this Measure, to extend or alter the time for holding any meeting or election or to modify the procedure laid down by this Measure in connection therewith;

(d) in any case in which there has been no valid choice to direct a fresh choice to be made, and to give such directions in connection therewith as he may think necessary; and

(e) in any case in which any difficulty arises, to give any directions which he may consider expedient for the purpose of removing the difficulty.

(2) The powers of the bishop under this section shall not enable him to validate anything that was invalid at the time it was done.

11 Savings

(1) Subject to section 9 above, nothing in this Measure shall be deemed to amend, repeal or affect any local act or any scheme made under any enactment affecting the churchwardens of a parish:

Provided that for the purposes of this Measure the Parish of Manchester Division Act 1850 (13 and 14 Vict. c. 41) shall be deemed to be a general act.

(2) Subject to section 12 below, in the case of any parish where there is an existing custom which regulates the number of church-wardens or the manner in which the churchwardens are chosen, nothing in this Measure shall affect that custom:

Provided that in the case of any parish where in accordance with that custom any churchwarden was, before the coming into force of the Churchwardens (Appointment and Resignation) Measure 1964 (No. 3), chosen by the vestry of that parish jointly with any other person or persons that churchwarden shall be chosen by the meeting of the parishioners jointly with the other person or persons.

12 Abolition of existing customs

(1) A meeting of the parishioners of a parish may pass a resolution abolishing any existing custom which regulates the number of churchwardens of the parish or the manner in which the churchwardens of the parish are chosen.

(2) Where any such resolution is passed the existing custom to which it relates shall cease to have effect on the date on which the next meeting of parishioners by which the churchwardens are to be elected is held.

(3) In the case of an existing custom which involves a person other than the minister in the choice of the churchwardens, a resolution under subsection (1) above shall not be passed without the written consent of that person.

13 Interpretation

(1) In this Measure, except in so far as the context otherwise requires –

'bishop' means the diocesan bishop concerned;

'existing custom' means a custom existing at the coming into force of this Measure which has continued for a period commencing before 1st January 1925;

'minister' has the same meaning as that assigned to that expression in rule 54(1) of the Church Representation Rules except that, where a special responsibility for pastoral care in respect of the parish in question has been assigned to a member of the team in a team ministry under section 20(8A) of the Pastoral Measure 1983 (1983 No. 1) but a special cure of souls in respect of the parish has not been assigned to a vicar in the team ministry by a scheme under that Measure or by his licence from the bishop, it means that member;

'pastoral scheme' has the same meaning as that assigned to that expression in section 87(1) of the Pastoral Measure 1983;

'actual communicant', 'parish' and 'public worship' have the same meanings respectively as those assigned to those expressions in rule 54(1) of the Church Representation Rules.

(2) Where by virtue of any custom existing at the coming into force of the Churchwardens (Appointment and Resignation)

Measure 1964 (1964 No. 3) the choice of a churchwarden was, under section 12(2) of that Measure, required to be made by the meeting of the parishioners jointly with another person or persons that custom shall be deemed to be an existing custom for the purposes of this Measure.

14 Transitional provisions
The transitional provisions in Schedule 1 to this Measure shall have effect.

15 Consequential amendment and repeals
(1) The enactment mentioned in Schedule 2 to this Measure shall have effect subject to the consequential amendment specified in that Schedule.

(2) The enactments mentioned in Schedule 3 to this Measure are hereby repealed to the extent specified in the third column of that Schedule.

16 Short title, commencement and extent
(1) This Measure may be cited as the Churchwardens Measure 2001.

(2) This Measure shall come into force on such day as the Archbishops of Canterbury and York may jointly appoint, and different days may be appointed for different provisions.

(3) This Measure shall extend to the whole of the Provinces of Canterbury and York except the Channel Islands and the Isle of Man, but the provisions thereof may be applied to the Channel Islands as defined in the Channel Islands (Church Legislation) Measures 1931 and 1957, or either of them, in accordance with those Measures and if an Act of Tynwald or an instrument made in pursuance of an Act of Tynwald so provides, shall extend to the Isle of Man subject to such exceptions, adaptations or modifications as may be specified in the Act of Tynwald or instrument.

Appendix 5

Resources for the churchwarden

(It is worth noting that so much information is available online that it makes sense for at least one out of every two churchwardens to have access to the Internet.)

A map of the parish
If there is not one available, contact the Church Commissioners, Church House, Great Smith Street, London SW1P 3AZ. A quick way to check boundaries is to use the *A church near you* website: <http://www.achurchnearyou.com/venue_search.php>.

Fees list
The Table of Parochial Fees is sent out to parish clergy by the Archbishops' Council; it gives the fees due both to the parish and to the incumbent or diocese for baptisms, weddings, funerals, register searches, etc. It can be downloaded from <http://www.cofe.anglican.org/lifeevents/fees/>.

Reference books
The Church of England Year Book
Crockford's Clerical Directory
The Diocesan Yearbook

All available from Church House Bookshop, 31 Great Smith Street, London SW1P 3BN; tel. 020 7799 4064; website <http://www.chbookshop.co.uk>.

Canons, Rules and Acts
The Canons of the Church of England: you can buy a copy or download them from <http://www.cofe.anglican.org/about/churchlawlegis/canons/>.

The Charities Act 1993 and the PCC, 3rd edition 2006, including
    church accounting regulations, is available from Church
    House Bookshop. The second edition, 2001, can also be
    downloaded from <http://www.cofe.anglican.org/info/papers/
    charact/charityact.pdf>.
Church Representation Rules: the latest edition came out in 2006,
    available from Church House Bookshop.
With effect from the first Church of England Measure of 1988, the
    full text of all new Church of England Measures is available
    via the web pages of the Office of Public Sector Information at
    <http://www.opsi.gov.uk/uk-church-measures/index.htm>.

Worship books
Book of Common Prayer
Common Worship
The Lectionary

Common Worship is a collection of texts, including commonly
used texts from the Book of Common Prayer and the 1928 Prayer
Book. It is available online at <http://www.cofe.anglican.org/
worship/liturgy/commonworship/texts/>.

All available from Church House Bookshop. See also <http://
www.cofe.anglican.org/worship/liturgy/commonworship>.

Websites
<http://www.anglicancommunion.org> is the website of the
    Anglican Communion. It contains plenty of news and
    resources.
<http://www.cafonline.org> is the Charities Aid Foundation's
    website, a worthwhile place to consult when fundraising.
<http://www.churchcare.co.uk> is a one-stop site for everything to
    do with church maintenance.
<http://www.churchnewspaper.com/?go=news> and <http://www.
    churchtimes.co.uk> take you to the online versions of the
    main church newspapers.
<http://www.cofe.anglican.org> is the main Church of England
    website. It contains a great deal of information, though not
    always in the most obvious places.

<http://www.dsc.org.uk> is the website for the Directory of Social Change, a good place to start with your fundraising research.

<http://www.ecclawsoc.org.uk/cases/index.shtml> and <http://journals.cambridge.org/action/displayJournal?jid=ELJ> have summaries of many of the legal cases reported in the *Journal of the Ecclesiastical Law Society*.

<http://www.hmrc.gov.uk/charities/gift_aid/> is the part of the HM Revenue and Customs' site where you can find details of how the Gift Aid scheme works.

Notes

1 M. Nolan, *A Treatise of the Laws for the Relief and Settlement of the Poor*, vol. 2, London, 1808, p. 180.
2 Nolan, *Treatise*, p. 228.
3 Ian Russell, *The Churchwarden's Handbook*, Stowmarket, Kevin Mayhew, 2000, p. 20.
4 W. S. Wigglesworth, 'The Office of Churchwarden', in A. E. J. Rawlinson, *The World's Question and the Christian Answer*, London, Longmans, 1944, p. 104.
5 NRSV.
6 Section 9(3).
7 Acts 1.23–6 (JB).
8 R. Bursell, *Liturgy, Order and the Law*, Oxford, Clarendon Press, 1996, p. 257.
9 In July 2003 the government initiated a review of the preliminaries to marriage and the method of registration which would involve the abolition of banns and marriage registers as we understand them. However, the proposed change to universal civil preliminaries to marriage has not been implemented.
10 Mark 1.35–7.
11 Luke 17.10 (AV).

Index